More Praise for *Uncovering the Life of Your Dreams*

"*Uncovering the Life of Your Dreams* is an insightful, enjoyable read. It opens us up to new perspectives about what reality is and how we co-create within it to find our purpose, move beyond our limitations, and create the fulfilling life we were meant to have."

—Howard Martin, co-author, *The HeartMath Solution* and *Heart Intelligence*, Executive Vice President, HeartMath Inc.

"A fascinating reflection on what really matters!"

—Marshall Goldsmith, New York Times #1 bestselling author of *Triggers, MOJO,* and *What Got You Here Won't Get You There*

"Bruce Schneider has achieved a rare alignment between lofty aspiration and practical reality, manifesting a life that is the expression of his dreams. In an original, entertaining, and compelling way, *Uncovering the Life of Your Dreams* shows how you can do this, too."

—Michael J. Gelb, author of *How to Think Like Leonardo da Vinci* and *The Art of Connection*

"*Uncovering the Life of Your Dreams* is a book that can't be read just once. I love the story and the playful way it introduces key concepts for a meaningful and joyful life. In sharing the concepts with my team, I've found that the book meets people where they are at and helps them on their personal development and leadership journeys."

—Simone Noordegraaf, Head of GBS Europe @ AkzoNobel, Amsterdam, The Netherlands

"I loved it! A unique and mesmerizing book that expands your creativity and awakens your inner genius."

—Dr. Joe Vitale, author of *Zero Limits* and
The Awakened Millionaire

"In my profession, faith is the difference between winning and losing. *Uncovering the Life of Your Dreams* offers not only faith, but also a unique process that can empower you to become the extraordinary person you were meant to be."

—Carlos Beltran, 9-time Major League Baseball All-Star

uncovering
the life *of*
your dreams

AN ENLIGHTENING STORY

bruce d schneider

WILEY

Library of Congress Cataloging-in-Publication Data:

Names: Schneider, Bruce D., author.
Title: Uncovering the life of your dreams : an enlightening story / Bruce D.
  Schneider.
Description: Hoboken : Wiley, 2018. |
Identifiers: LCCN 2018001197 (print) | LCCN 2018004613 (ebook) | ISBN
  9781119469049 (pdf) | ISBN 9781119469032 (epub) | ISBN 9781119469094
  (cloth)
Subjects: LCSH: Spiritual life. | Self-acceptance–Religious aspects. |
  Self-realization–Religious aspects.
Classification: LCC BL624 (ebook) | LCC BL624 .S3553 2018 (print) | DDC
  204/.4–dc23
LC record available at https://lccn.loc.gov/2018001197

Printed in the United States of America

10 9 8 7 6 5 4 3 2 1

To the iPEC coaches and other members of the OneIdeaAway.com community, who help people uncover and then live the life of their dreams.

Acknowledgments

With Gratitude to . . .

Liz Fisch, for too many things to mention here, except your tremendous talents and effort in making this book what it is.

iPEC CEO Joan Ryan, President Luke Iorio, and colleague Monica Coleman, for your support, partnership, and important contributions.

iPEC's marketing team, who worked tirelessly to create the life-changing OneIdeaAway.com community: Heather Doyle, Michael Robinson, Cassandra Gaddis, Erika Schneider, Jenny Wiley, Jordan Page, Laura Kunzie, Rachel Hurley, and Shaunlee Hostutler.

iPEC's co-owners, partners, trainers, and mentors, as well as my friends and family who helped in the creation of this book. Whether you gave feedback on a preview copy, were the inspiration for a character, or played another role, know that my gratitude is unending. Though this list is long, it is not all-inclusive, as it would take another book to fully honor all the amazing people who deserve to be recognized for their presence in my life:

Amina Hedayat, Anabel Francisco, Andy Zundel, Angela Stanford, Anissa Matthews, Ascanio Pignatelli, Barb Newton, Barbara Anselmi, Barbara Curatolo, Barbra Schneider, Bill Bent, Bill Sex, Bridgette Simmonds, Cheryl Johns, Cheryl Neville, Chris Finnegan,

Christie Koenigsmark, Christine Kloser, Christine Rodek, Christine Scantland, Cindy DuSair, Cindy Gardner, Cory Katuna, Craig Schneiderman, Dan Beldowicz, Daniel Macca, Debbie Bercume, Debbie Jaques, Debby Lott, Deborah Degner, Deborah Van de Grift, Demetra Moore, Don Madura, Ed Abel, Francine Carter, Gary Fisch, Gary Kamen, Gianina Monroe, Grace Germond, Heidi Krantz, Jacqui Neurauter, Jaimini Chandarana, Janelle Anderson, Jeff Gitterman, Jennifer Kwiatowski, Jennifer Potthoff, Jerry Schneiderman, Jessica Barreira, Jessica Beltran, John Bond, Joseph Maqqar, Joy Humbarger, Joyce Schneiderman, Karen Osgood, Kathleen Avery, Kellie De Ruyter, Kimberly Bagwell, Kim Connor, Kyle Pertuis, Laurie Lawson, Lawrence Lussier, Lesley Picchietti, Lisa Kaplin, Lisa Te Slaa, Lou Iorio, Lynn Waldorf, Maria Maduri, Maria Monroe, Mark Schall, Mary Jo Rathgeb, Mel Cockerham, Michael Berning, Michael Fisch, Micheline Germanos, Mindy Szeto, Nick Kolesnikoff, Nina Cashman, Paul Monroe, Peter Curtis, Raechel Anderson Dressler, Ronne Ozgu, Russell Gibson, Ryan Stanley, Sandra Slough, Sara and Zac Moskowitz, Shelley Pernot, Sherry Dutra, Sherri Gerek, Sheryl James, Simone Nordegraff, Sonia Lopez, Stacy Campesi, Stacy Hartmann, Stephanie Marisca, Steve Coleman, Susan King, Susan Stone, Suzanne Reilley, Tamarra Robinson, Tambre Leighn, Tara Roth, Taylor Laquaglia, Teresa and Tony Curatolo, Teresa Brenke, Terry Fralich, Theresa Horezga, Theresa Murphy, Tonya Echols, Tyler Caccavale, Wendy Stantzos, and Zack Lemelle.

Finally, the team at John Wiley & Sons—Editor Shannon Vargo, Peter Knox, Kelly Martin, Vicki Adang, and Deborah Schindlar—for your belief in the project and for helping to make this dream a reality.

Preface

When I was 19 years old, a drunk driver killed himself and nearly me by driving the wrong direction down a highway. I survived the head-on collision, but not as the same person I was before it. It's been decades since that accident, and I can still vividly recall the grueling pain of my battered body and, at the same time, the unimaginable and extraordinary experience of knowing that I was something other than that body—something beyond words and perhaps even beyond worlds. After the accident, I was awakened to a new reality, one in which figuring out who I really was and why I was still here became the focus of my existence.

Over the past 40 years, I have searched for the answer to those questions, as well as countless others. Through meditation and dreaming, the latter often of the lucid variety, I've developed a process I've termed "uncovery," that is, removing all that is mind-fabricated until only purity remains. The uncovery process requires first questioning everything, especially that which is considered to be reality, and then continually identifying and eliminating any ego-generated thoughts or beliefs that cloud or distort what is truly real. This journey to higher consciousness has helped me chip away at all of the things that I am not to uncover the truth of who I truly am. While I did not necessarily find the answers, I certainly found my answers.

This book tells the story of a character named Scott Billings. Like you and me, Scott wants to know his true nature so that he can lead a more meaningful, purposeful, and fulfilling life.

I wrote this book as a narrative to help you, the reader, more easily step into Scott's shoes so that you can uncover more about the meaning and purpose of your life. All of Scott's adventures are based on my actual experiences. I hope that, in sharing them, a door is opened for you to experience something different—perhaps, as was the case with me, something extraordinary.

My purpose in life is not to teach, preach, or convince anyone of anything, but instead to empower others to seek their own answers, access their true dreams, and overcome anything that gets in the way of making those dreams a reality.

If you'd like to uncover the life you've been waiting for, perhaps what you seek is only a dream away . . .

uncovering
the life *of*
your dreams

Now: Setting the Stage

Sooner or later you will awaken to realize that you've spent nearly your entire life worrying about things you could not control, bothered by insignificant annoyances, and distracted by self-inflicted challenges.

On that day, you will also realize that you've missed seeing a beautiful and entertaining world; a world filled with mystery, suspense, drama, comedy, and an unlimited opportunity to engage in and fully appreciate the human experience.

Hopefully, that day will come soon, because when it does, you will smile as your body fills with a warmth that you will recognize as joy, and you will be incredibly grateful that you are alive and can choose how you want to spend the rest of your life.

Six months ago, before my journey began, I would have never thought I'd find myself sitting in the middle of an abandoned playhouse wearing a Bruce Springsteen tee shirt, a thin polka-dotted necktie, a pair of torn Levi's jeans with a magnifying glass in one of the pockets, a pair of broken sandals, and a fisherman's hat. And I'd certainly never have imagined that in this darkened room

1

on this astonishing day, I would be about to open my eyes to a miracle.

Sitting here, I realize that my world had previously been a prison that kept me sleepwalking through life, ignorant and blind. Blind to the truth about reality, about life, about who I truly was. Now, with my eyes closed, I can see more clearly than ever before and in a few moments, after the count of three, I will open my eyes and see the absolute truth.

The answer to life's most important question is about to be answered, yet for the first time in my life, I'm content just sitting here, eyes closed.

Surreal and perfect. I'm smiling the kind of smile people have when they meet their soul mate for the first time and just know they have been, and will be, together, forever.

What will I see? I don't know, and I have no expectations. I'm just ready—ready to open my eyes to an even deeper reality.

Literally, I didn't see this coming.

1 . . .

I am ready.

2 . . .

What a journey . . .

Six Months Earlier: Scott's Journey

There are many garden paths.

On each, there are beautiful flowers to pick.

A particular path may not be yours,

but do take the flowers with you when you leave.

1

From where I spent most of my time—which was sitting at a desk next to a large, metal-framed window in my third-floor office at DM Realty—the streets of New York looked like a scene out of an old storybook. It wasn't always a pleasant scene, but the distraction of staring at the constant activity below helped to take my mind off my empty life.

For as long as I could remember, I had been searching for some answers to make sense of it all. There were many questions to which I wanted the answers, yet every time I thought about my life, I found myself constantly returning to one question in particular: Is this all there is?

One afternoon in late fall, while staring out the window of my office and contemplating that question, I gave up on finding the answer. I can't explain why it happened then. All I know is that I came to the conclusion that there *was* no satisfying answer—no purpose to or meaning for my life. No purpose for anyone else's, either. Nothing more than this.

I decided to stop trying to figure it out and admitted to myself that my search for answers was simply an exercise to assuage my fear that life was meaningless. At that moment of resignation, I decided to accept that life was just a random, mathematical, and biological evolutionary process. A miracle, of course, that it could happen, but a meaninglessness miracle, nevertheless.

One might think that finally coming to any conclusion would bring some level of relief. Instead, the only thing I sensed was loss that this was, indeed, all there was to the waste of time that I called life. At that moment, I felt completely without hope.

It was just then that my boss walked in.

"Scott!" he yelled, loudly enough to let everyone else in the office know he was there and he was unhappy. I turned quickly to respond.

"I'm . . . I . . . Damon, I was just thinking about the Concord account. I'm developing a strategy."

"Really? Looks like you're just wasting time. Like usual. I don't know why I even gave you that lead. If it wasn't for Karine . . ." he blurted out, stopping there and closing his eyes briefly, as if to redirect his thoughts. "You need to decide if you really want this job, once and for all."

I didn't know what to say, and he didn't give me much of a chance to come up with something.

"You know, there was a time when nothing could stop you from getting what you wanted. Now, you don't seem to care about anything."

He didn't wait for a response to that, either. He just turned and walked out of the room into the hallway, where my administrative assistant, Karine, who had clearly listened to the whole thing, quickly looked away as he moved past her and across the floor to his office down the hall.

Damon's personality had certainly changed since I'd first met him. He'd turned into a moody guy with little patience—not at all like the person he used to be when we were in college together or even who he'd been just a few years earlier, before he took over the company from his father.

But he was right, of course. I wasn't working on—or even thinking about—the Concord account. I didn't know why he gave me the lead, either. I wasn't even sure why he hadn't already fired me. We both knew I'd lost my passion for the job and that I was little more than a charity case. I didn't know what, if anything, would have to happen to re-engage me, not only in my career but in my life as well.

And then a real miracle happened. Well, that's when it began, anyway. I know exactly what time it was: 2:13 p.m. I remember that specific time because on that cool Tuesday afternoon in November, something unusual caught my attention. A flash of bright light reflected off the wall clock and back into my eyes, causing me to shield them with my arm.

I scanned the room for the source of the light and realized it was coming through the window from outside. Perhaps it was just a reflection from the sun at that particular time of the day, but it was definitely not something that I had ever seen before. I stood and looked outside and saw a steady, almost blinding, bright beam coming from a single spot across the street on the sidewalk, shining directly into my office.

Like a moth to a flame, from somewhere within the depth of my body, I suddenly felt a powerful tingling sensation and a strong, almost magnetic, pull toward the light. I rushed out of my office, startling Karine. She started to say something to me, but her words faded as I headed into the stairwell, not wanting to wait for the elevator. Afraid the light might disappear by the time I got outside, I took the stairs, a few at a time, as my anticipation grew.

When I made it to the lobby, I stopped for a second to orient myself. I looked across the street, and the light was still there.

As I made my way toward the light, its brightness dimmed. I thought I was imagining that, so I stopped midstride and began to take a few steps backward. I was probably a sight to see, not to mention an accident waiting to happen, and one would have if not for some resourceful driving by one of New York's cabbies. I barely noticed the cab, though, for I was mesmerized by how the light grew brighter with each step I took *away* from it. I started heading in the direction of the light again, but by the time I reached the other side of the street, the light was nearly completely gone.

A few people walked past me as I made my way. I looked into each of their faces for some sign that they, too, saw this strange light. No one else seemed to notice anything unusual. The fall air was quite chilly, and watching a passerby reach down to zip up his child's jacket made me realize I hadn't grabbed my coat in my hasty exit. I was thinking about turning back when a gust of wind slapped that thought away, and I again focused only on finding the source of the light.

I slowly edged closer and saw an elderly man holding a white cardboard sign. While I couldn't make out what was written on the sign, when I tilted my head a little, I could see a slight glimmer coming off of it. I guessed the sign was indeed reflecting sunlight that, from my vantage point, I was unable to see.

The man was about 5'6" tall, with salt-and-pepper hair. He was dressed in ragged clothing, and I was pretty sure he was cold. From where I was standing, I couldn't see into the bucket on the ground in front of him to tell if anyone had given money to this poor freezing soul.

Despite his appearance, there was something different about the man. Although he appeared to be panhandling, he had picked an oddly disadvantageous location on the edge of the curb in the middle of the block. Since he was facing the street, pedestrians walking by would see only his back, and because he was not near the corner, he could not approach cars stopped for red lights. I thought twice about approaching further, but my intrigue got the better of me and I continued to move closer.

The light was now completely gone, and I could see the sign clearly. It was blank. It was just a blank white sign, held up by a homeless man standing the wrong way on a street in midtown Manhattan.

I leaned in and said hello, but he neither responded to nor acknowledged me. I found myself uncertain of what to do next, but then the thought popped into my head to give him some money. *Not too much money,* I thought, *but a sum that would hopefully get a reaction from him.* I reached into my wallet, took out a ten-dollar bill and extended my arm. He didn't move. I leaned in to look into the bucket and saw that it was empty. I thought about just dropping the bill into it and leaving, but decided to try to engage him by continuing to offer him the bill. For as long as I could, I held my arm extended toward him, bill in hand. I couldn't tell how much time had passed, but when I started to feel my fingers grow numb from the cold, I gave up and put the money in the bucket. I looked at him, again waiting for some sort of acknowledgment. But there was nothing. No glance, no smile, no nod, no thank you. Nothing. Not even a flinch. I thought to myself, *I'm an idiot. Damon is going to flip out if he finds out I left the office. I need to get back to work. Maybe I'll get lucky and he won't have noticed that I was gone.*

As I turned away from the man and took a step back toward my office, he started to speak.

"I feel your pain," I heard behind me in a rather deep, monotone, and hoarse voice. The broken silence startled me and I immediately felt crushing waves of fear and grief. I felt the urge to get away as quickly as I could but couldn't seem to move.

It took a few moments to collect myself enough to face him and respond. "Are you talking to me?" I asked quietly and cautiously. Since I had been turned away from him when I heard the voice, the thought occurred to me that maybe it wasn't me he was addressing or perhaps it wasn't even him who had spoken.

"Who are you?" he asked. Looking around, I saw no one but the two of us.

"I'm . . . I work across the street," I said, reflexively pointing to my office window. He didn't look up. "I noticed a light outside my window. It was coming from over here. Did . . . did you see it?"

"Yes."

A man of few words, I presumed. "And who are you?"

"I am the beggar," he responded. "I am *a* beggar" would have made more sense to me, but I decided not to read into his choice of words.

"What was the pain you were talking about?" I asked but had a feeling what was coming was a blank stare—which was exactly what I got. I also knew the answer to my question. All my life I'd been afraid. It was an underlying fear that seemed to always be there, ready to strike at the worst possible moments. Be it with regard to a job, relationship, opportunity, or challenge, I always felt a painful and almost crippling fear that made me feel that I was just not good enough to accomplish anything great. Sometimes I found enough courage to face a challenge in spite of it, but most other times, not. Regardless of what action I took, the feeling was pervasive. I believed I'd done a pretty good job of hiding this fear, and in turn accomplishing enough to achieve a decent life, but right now, in front of a total stranger, I felt like I was an open book and that he'd chosen to read the only chapter I desperately wanted to remain closed.

He turned his head as if to stare deep into my soul. Although I still felt fear somewhere within me, I also felt something completely different from anything I'd ever experienced. A wave of energy ran through me—a low-voltage and enjoyable roll of energy through-out my entire body from my feet to my head. Suddenly, I felt as if I was not on a city street with him; we were transported somewhere else. I didn't know where I was or what was happening. I was still right there, but I was also not there.

He grabbed the lapels of his coat and, as if showing me his heart, opened his coat for a brief moment. As he did, the fear within me completely disappeared. Tears began to well up in my eyes, and I felt no need to wipe them away. For a moment, I felt powerful, clear, and focused. It was then I realized that he was not a beggar, nor was he an old man. I wasn't certain that he was mortal and was even less certain that he was actually standing there with me. His age and clothing didn't change, nor did anything else about him, yet when I looked past his soiled coat and the dirt caked in the crevices of his face, I realized that he was glowing. It was absolutely beautiful. Stunning. He was the source of the light that I saw; it was not the sign, not from the sun, and perhaps not even from this world.

He closed his shabby coat, and though I could no longer see the light coming directly from his body, I could feel its warmth deep within me. I wasn't expecting to be outside this long, yet I was no longer cold. In fact, I felt warm and strong, and I felt that I could, and part of me wanted to, stand there forever.

"I am humbled to be with you," I said. I had a million questions, but only one came out of my mouth. "May I ask you why the sign is blank?"

"It is because most people do not want to know what it says," he responded.

"I do," I retorted.

"Then why do you see a blank sign?" he asked curiously, without any hint of judgment.

Gusts of wind so strong they could have knocked me off balance began whipping around, but the air between us was still, and I felt steady. I closed my eyes before responding, "The sign is filled with messages." That didn't sound like something I would say. I had the weird thought that he was talking *through* me, as if he was speaking using my mind and my voice and I didn't have control over what I was saying.

The beggar continued where I left off. "It is up to you to decide when and what you are ready or willing to see. There are signs, everywhere, and it's your choice to read them or not and then determine what they mean to you. So what *does* this sign mean to you?"

I responded, again with words that didn't sound like my own. "I think you, showing up here as a beggar, offer me the opportunity to realize that I am not what I appear to be, as I know you are not who you appear to be."

"I am the beggar," he reiterated.

"No, I mean . . . I know you are . . . but you really aren't, right?" I said, believing that I was now owning my words again.

He didn't answer and instead asked another question.

"Why do you suppose I beg?"

"You probably . . ." I stopped myself at that point, realizing that anything I said next would sound condescending or judgmental.

"I do not beg for money, and I do not beg for me," he said. "I beg for you. I beg for you to give me money."

"Why?" I asked.

"Because that is what I do," he patiently responded.

I could have probed more but decided it would have been unproductive to do so. I didn't understand any of what was happening, and surprisingly, I didn't feel I needed to.

I thought of asking him how he dealt with the cold and wind, but having felt the warmth of his light, I figured that I already knew the answer. "I know you're making a statement, but aren't you afraid that someone will harm you? Can't you get your message across in another way?"

"I have. Many times, and in many ways. The message is always there for anyone who is ready to receive it. And I am safe. What can people take from me? My money? I do not have any. My clothes? Who would want them? My body? Someone might take it one day, and if so, so be it. My body would be still, but I would still be."

What he said should have saddened me, but instead it felt comforting. I imagined it was difficult living like that and wondered why he would choose to do so if he didn't have to. Yet I had the feeling he wanted to, as if he was born to do so.

And then he continued, "You don't have to feel the suffering of your fear. I can do that for the both of us." With that, he turned away from me and once again stared ahead.

I knew I wasn't ready to fully grasp his message, so I didn't try. I also knew he was right about my suffering. But in that moment, I wasn't ready to explore that pain. Instead, I chose to dwell within the amazing and deepening sensations and emotions that seemed both brand new yet familiar to me. It was as if the beggar gave me a long-desired and welcome reprieve from myself.

I took a long deep breath and felt the wind flow though my body. It felt a part of me, everything did, as if I was complete and whole but now not limited to my body. There was only that moment, and no other time or place in the universe existed. In the middle of the block on that Tuesday afternoon in a windstorm, I was home. Safe, fearless, invulnerable.

"That's enough for now," he said.

I knew at that moment that the bliss I felt would end and that I would strive to feel it again, so his statement offered a possibility. "You said 'for now.' Does that mean that I can meet with you again?"

"What you seek is only a dream away," he said in a fading whisper.

His words seemed like another wind, one that blew me into an even deeper state of being. I completely lost myself, feeling my eyes close and my breath grow shallow. In that moment, all thoughts stopped. I was no thing. I was every thing.

I probably stood motionless in that spot for quite some time. When I opened my eyes, the beggar was no longer in front of me. I looked around until I saw caught a glimpse of him moving between other passersby, walking down the street with the sign in one hand and the bucket in the other.

2

Back in my office, I texted my friend Larry to see if he could meet for dinner. I couldn't wait to tell him what had happened.

I'd met Larry in middle school. Back then I was thin and very introverted. The combination made me an easy target for bullies.

Between classes one afternoon, I was taking a drink at the hallway water fountain when one of the school's worst bullies, Chris Flaggart, held my head down on the spigot to the point where I felt like I was drowning. I flailed my arms in panic, but he wouldn't let me go. I can still hear him laughing and saying, "I think he's thirsty," to a few kids who laughed as well. I was in complete shock and was sure I was going to die. He let me go suddenly, and I fell to the floor, gasping for breath. I woke up in the nurse's office.

"Are you okay?" the nurse asked. I could hear her but couldn't speak yet. After a little while, I managed to nod and then eventually sat up in the infirmary bed.

"Do you remember what happened?" she asked, looking squarely at me.

"I . . . I'm not sure," I said, looking away, my first thought being not to rat Chris out because things would be worse if I did.

"Well, I heard Chris Flaggart pushed your head into the water fountain," she replied, already knowing the sequence of events.

"Does that sound right?" Before I could respond, she continued, "Your friend Larry Phillips came along and intervened. I don't think you have to worry about Mr. Flaggart bothering you again."

I didn't know what to say. Larry Phillips was not my friend. In fact, I didn't even know him. I knew of him—everyone did. He was one of the few black kids at our school. Larry seemed to be a boy in a man's body who was even more of an introvert than I was. He always sat alone at lunch. But I never had the courage to sit near or speak to him because he was an intimidating figure.

"Well, I think you're going to be okay," the nurse said, interrupting my thoughts. "You'd better get back to class."

* * *

I passed Larry in the hall a few times over the next week but was too nervous to speak with him. He just walked by me, seemingly without any recognition, and I wondered if he even knew it was me he had rescued. A week after that, I sat close to him during lunch, but not near enough to make either one of us uncomfortable. I tentatively waited until he made eye contact. He pointed his finger to me, mouthed the word "you," and smiled. Then he went back to eating. I moved closer, sat down, and quietly muttered, "Thank you for the other day."

"For what?" he asked.

"For helping me out with Chris."

"Oh that? Yeah. I don't like bullies," was all he said.

"Can I ask you a question?" He looked up. "Why don't you like to eat lunch with anyone?"

"No one wants to eat lunch with me, Scott."

I was pleasantly surprised that he knew my name, but his statement was one of the saddest things I had ever heard.

We finished lunch together, in silence.

From that day on, Larry and I were inseparable. I discovered him to be gentle, wise, and kind. We spent a lot of time together, playing sports and just hanging out. Even though Larry was bigger than I was, I was more athletic and almost always better in whatever sport we played. He never cared, and neither did I. Regardless of the results of a game, he'd just point his finger at me and say "you," just as he did that first time at the lunch table.

The thing Larry was much better at than I was, though, was relationships. His lasted a lot longer than mine usually did, and he eventually married an old flame from grad school. I wasn't so lucky. But he would always encourage me to find something more than the short-term relationships in which I always seemed to wind up. He was a real friend, a true best friend. When I reached for the phone, it was almost always Larry I'd be calling or texting.

My phone buzzed as Larry's reply arrived. "Ginette and Paula are doing some college research, so yeah, I'm free. Las Puertas, 7:30. See you then." Las Puertas was located a few blocks from my office, and even though Larry lived in the Bronx, it was our favorite restaurant, so we often met there.

I spent the rest of the afternoon staring out my office window. I could still feel some of the warmth within me, but it was fading fast. I was unsure of what had happened to me or how I would even begin to tell Larry about it.

* * *

I had my coat on during my walk to the cafe, yet I was still cold. In fact, by then I couldn't feel any of the warmth or tranquility that I had felt earlier, so I began to seriously question whether the whole thing actually occurred. I knew what I felt, and the experience of that feeling was something I'd always remember. I just didn't know if the event that caused that feeling really happened. I had the depressing thought that maybe I had just been daydreaming or had fallen asleep in my office. I could not even recall what happened after my encounter with the beggar. I just found myself back in my office with no idea how I got there. I considered asking Karine if I had actually left the building but was too embarrassed to do that.

Las Puertas was a friendly, quiet restaurant that served the only authentic Puerto Rican cuisine in midtown. The tables were decorated with brightly colored paper placemats depicting maps of San Juan and its surrounding areas. I had visited Puerto Rico with a girlfriend a few years earlier, and my love for Puerto Rican food endured, even though that relationship didn't survive the flight home. Las Puertas was my frequent lunch stop, and I would visit it on occasion for dinner. That night was definitely an occasion. Either a miracle had occurred, or I needed to see a shrink.

Larry was already there seated at our usual table, which wasn't hard to secure, as the place was never busy and the waitress knew where we liked to sit. Upon greeting me, she would always say, with a slight and cute accent, "Right this way, *compañero*."

Larry was all smiles as he gave me a quick finger point and said "youuuu." I didn't respond; I just sat down in a daze and took a sip of the piña colada that was already waiting for me. Larry usually made fun of what he called my "girlie drink," but this time he probably sensed that I wasn't in the mood for teasing.

"You alright?" he asked.

I parted my mouth as if to say something, but just sat there, mouth open, slowly shaking my head back and forth.

"I'm confused. Your text sounded like something great happened, but you don't look like it did. What's going on?"

I exhaled loudly. "Something amazing might have happened today. I'm just not sure it actually happened or how to describe it."

The left side of Larry's closed mouth stretched into a comforting grin, and he nodded as if to say, "Whatever it is, I'm with you." Larry's ability to listen was extraordinary. That's one of the reasons I often confided in him. I knew he wouldn't judge me and also knew he would sit there all night without saying another word if that's what I needed in order to process.

I started from the very beginning—when Damon barged into my office. Larry knew Damon well. We all went to college together, and Damon was my freshman roommate. Larry roomed in the dorm next to us, and then the three of us pledged the same fraternity, Phi Alpha Delta. We hung out a lot together at the house and got quite close. After college, Larry decided to be a teacher, and Damon took a job at his family's real estate firm and got me a job there, too.

I recounted seeing the light and meeting the beggar as best I could, still unable to find the words to accurately describe what happened on the street. As I told the story, I realized that although he had used the word himself, "beggar" just didn't feel right. Larry listened to the entire story without interrupting. Even though I knew he was an amazingly accepting friend, I still looked for some judgment in his reactions as I spoke. When I finished, he just smiled again and waited a few moments before speaking.

"Fascinating," he began. "So, what do you think actually happened?"

"I really don't know," I said. "Honestly, I've just been trying to figure out if I've gone insane."

He smiled and said, "Leaving the question of your sanity aside for the moment . . ." He paused and flashed a grin to make sure I recognized that he was joking. "I know you don't know for sure, but at least tell me what you're thinking."

My eyes scanned the room, as if I was looking for the answer. I refocused on him and began speculating. "Okay, if I have to be honest . . ."

"You do," he said, with another comforting grin.

I continued. "I think there are a couple of possibilities. It could have been a daydream, I guess. It's also possible I was seeing things. I've been under a lot of stress lately, and I think my job is in jeopardy. Maybe I should go back to seeing that therapist, Jean. That probably wouldn't be a bad idea."

I paused, lost in thought, until I caught myself and went on. "I think she might be able to help me. I just want to rule out stress as the cause of a possible hallucination." I didn't really know what I was blabbing about right then, except that I was trying to convince him, and even more myself, that I should talk to somebody.

"Got it. See the therapist. Makes sense. You said a couple of possibilities; what's another one?" he asked, leaning in and putting his elbows on the table.

"Uhhh, well, I guess there's still the possibility that it really happened, in which case I would think . . . well . . . I wouldn't know what to think."

"Okay, here's my take on it. Regardless of what actually happened, I believe you had a powerful experience. And it doesn't matter whether it actually happened or you imagined it, because it was real to you. Figure out what you need to figure out, but in any case, know that you did experience something amazing. What could you take from the experience that could help you right now?"

I sat back and thought through what Larry was asking. "Well, I guess I'll never look at a homeless person in the same way again. I mean, you can never know truly who someone is, can you?" Larry nodded silently, which meant that I needed to keep speaking. "And . . . I know what I felt. You're right. It was real to me, regardless of anything else. I felt it, Lar. I think I felt . . . heaven. Maybe even God. I don't know if I'll figure anything else out, but I know I felt something awesome."

He did the finger point thing again and then reached to high-five me. Right before our hands met we both stopped, wiggled our fingers, turned our upper bodies to the right while pulling our hands back toward ourselves into a hitchhiker's position. This is something we used to do in college. Every once in a while, we still did the "Phi Five."

"Okay. What else?" he asked.

"The last thing I heard—only a dream away. I think there's something to that. I need to figure it out. Maybe it was literal. I mean, maybe I can feel what I felt again in my dreams, although, I'm not even sure if I dream. I never remember any of my dreams."

"Maybe there's a way you can. Ever heard of lucid dreaming?" Larry asked. "It's when you know you're dreaming, like being awake while you dream. I'm sure if you could do that you would remember them."

"Never heard of it," I said.

He suggested we look into it to learn more. Another great thing about Larry was his use of the word "we" when normally you'd expect to hear "you." I agreed to do some research on it and let him know what I found.

I got out of my seat and put my coat on. He didn't follow suit. "Let's go," I said.

Larry let out a deep belly laugh that got the attention of the few other people in the restaurant. "Dude, we didn't eat yet!" I sat down, a little embarrassed, as I took off my jacket.

3

"What you seek is only a dream away" was the phrase I kept muttering to myself as I settled into my apartment that evening. Located on the Upper East Side, my one-bedroom place was small but well lit and well appointed, thanks to a talented decorator I ended up dating for a short while.

"A dream away . . ." I wondered if the message was indeed literal, that I'd perhaps learn something while I slept, maybe even that night. My next thought was how horrible it would be to learn the meaning of life but then wake up without any memory of it. That's when I remembered Larry's mention of lucid dreaming.

I grabbed my iPad and googled the term. Over three million results. Wikipedia said that "A lucid dream is a dream during which the dreamer is aware of dreaming. During lucid dreaming, the dreamer may be able to exert some degree of control over the dream characters, narrative, and environment." *Okay*, I thought to myself, *this might be the right path. Maybe this is what the beggar meant.*

Trying to narrow down the results, I typed in "lucid dream workshops near me." I much preferred experiential learning to most other methods, so attending a face-to-face workshop felt right. On page two of the search, I saw an advertisement for a workshop at a nearby center, but it was another one outside the city that caught my attention and spoke directly to me. "Learn how to wake up in your dreams" was obvious enough, and then after a few more bullets, "Learn how to find the answers you're looking for." As soon as I read that, I got a strange but comforting chill, and I became aware of something within me that, without words, said, "This is it." I ended my research and called Larry.

"Sorry. I know it's late, but you won't believe the description of a workshop I just found." I could feel a level of excitement building. Since my experience earlier that day, I had felt very little of anything but confusion.

"Cool. When is it?" he asked, getting to the point.

"Uh . . . looks like next week. Tuesday night. Want to come with me?

"Let me check." I heard a muffled conversation in the background as he consulted Ginette. "I can't, sorry. Paula has a recital that night."

"No big deal. I'll still go. I'm a big boy." I still had some pride left.

"Good!" he said. "I think it's a great step for you. Maybe you'll even meet your dream woman there." This led to Larry's second belly laugh in only a couple of hours.

"Oh boy," I said. "That's quite brilliant and equally as disturbing." He laughed even louder. I heard Ginette's voice behind him whisper something, after which he said he had to go.

* * *

The next week flew by uneventfully. Each night, I willed myself to dream, and each morning, I tried to recall if I'd had a dream. I still couldn't remember having a single one.

At work, it felt like Damon had been avoiding me since the day of the "incident," and I was still unmotivated to get anything done. Even though I was still very curious and somewhat excited about the dream workshop, I thought that it was still life as usual. "Still life." I pondered the term and figured it was just about right. I dialed Karine's extension.

"Can you come into the office?" I asked. "Sure," she said, unenthusiastically. A few moments later, she walked into my office wearing a tight skirt and low-cut blouse.

The "sexretary" was the nickname people around the office gave her, and the clothing she wore didn't help change that image. I felt badly about that nickname and knew it wasn't appropriate, but I never stood up to the other idiots in the office to defend her. I just didn't want the confrontation. Mostly, the people in the office just left me alone, which I preferred.

I felt that Karine and I had a unique and mutually beneficial relationship. Even though she didn't overtly show it, I believed that she genuinely liked me. And even though she had the reputation she did, she was always very professional and proper with me.

Karine earned more than the typical administrative assistant, but that's because she was as far from typical as possible. At some point, we had kind of switched roles. I started doing all the back-end work, and she would meet with clients and prospects instead of me. Over the years, the introvert in me grew to hate talking to people I didn't know, while she was really good at it. I really didn't know if she actually knew anything about what she was doing, but the clients seemed to like her, a lot, and I didn't ask why. Regardless of how she did it, I knew that Karine was the best salesperson in the entire company.

"Thanks, Karine. Listen, I know you are well aware of how important this account is for the company, and I want to make sure you are prepared. So, what can I do to help you with that?"

"I think I got it. It'll be good. You don't have to worry," she said.

She always said the same exact thing. I counted on it, as I doubted I could help her, anyway. Karine never complained about anything. I assumed she enjoyed her job and was happy with the arrangement. To show my appreciation, I once bought her a pearl bracelet, and she wore it every day.

She left the office without any other conversation.

* * *

Tuesday evening finally arrived, and I left work early to get a bite to eat at Las Puertas before heading to the workshop. The waitress was friendly as usual, and unfortunately the place was empty as usual, as well. "Where are all the customers? The food is excellent here," I asked.

She shrugged her shoulders and, in her slightly detectible accent, she said, "I don't know, *compañero*." I didn't know, either. In fact, except for my expertise in the eating end of it, I knew nothing about the restaurant business. So, I just ordered my favorite dish, *arroz blanco con habichuelas y pollo guisado*, a mildly spicy combination of chicken, rice, and beans. I devoured it, paid the bill, and left for the workshop.

After a thirty-minute cab ride, I stood in front of an old stone building that had probably been used as a grammar school years ago and was now home of the Ann Marie Casman Center for Holistic Education. I walked into the lobby, checked in at the reception desk, and spent some time checking out the list of upcoming workshops before heading up the old and creaking stairwell to a fairly small classroom. The chairs were set up theater style, with four seats across and four rows back. I chose a seat in the third row, behind most of the half-dozen others there. In the front of the room, a thin man, dressed very professionally and probably in his late sixties, was attempting to get a projector to work.

The presenter, who introduced himself as Tom Reynolds, began. "Welcome," he said. "Today we're going to explore the world of lucid dreaming. I just love this topic, and think you'll find it quite eye-opening, until you go to bed that is, in which case keeping your eyes open will definitely get in the way of the process," he snickered. Other than a couple of grins, the participants were silent. He continued with a warm and engaging smile. "Sorry about that, couldn't help myself. So, before we get going, I'd like all of you to briefly introduce yourselves and tell us the one thing you hope to gain from tonight's workshop."

I only half-listened to most of the answers, thinking about what I'd say when it was my turn. *What could I say, anyway? That I'm here because a beggar told me that what I am seeking is but a dream away? Or that I'm questioning my sense of reality? Nah.* I just said, "My name is Scott, and I just want to know more about lucid dreaming." Clearly not very original or deep, but at least no one thought I was crazy. Well, except me, perhaps.

The guy sitting next to me, Alex, was the last to go. Without any hesitation on his part, he announced that he wanted to learn to have sex in his dreams. *Really?* I thought. *And I was worried about seeming crazy?* As I pondered what he said, however, I considered that, since I hadn't even been out on a date in a while, the notion of having sex in my dreams didn't really sound like such a crazy idea.

"Thank you all for sharing," Tom said. "Let's start with a guided meditation." He turned off most of the lights and invited us to close our eyes and to get comfortable. I wasn't entirely sure how comfortable I'd be with my eyes closed and Alex in close proximity, so I kept one eye slightly open, mostly just curiously, to see what he would do.

I heard a noise and turned toward it. My one half-open eye focused on a new workshop attendee who had just walked into the room. I opened both eyes enough to get a clearer view. He was wearing light gray pants, a dark gray sweatshirt, and a black baseball cap that covered his eyes with its brim. He was holding what seemed to be a book in his right hand.

He walked right past me, and when he did, I felt a different kind of chill than the pleasant one I'd felt when I'd read about the workshop. This one was like a deep shiver, almost painful, causing the hairs on my arms to stand up. He sat directly behind me where I couldn't see him at all. I was seriously frightened and couldn't wait until we were done with the meditation so the lights would again brighten the room.

Finally, we all opened our eyes, and the lights came back up. Tom told us to stand up and stretch a bit, and I did so, trying to look casual as I glanced at all the others in the room. When I looked the stranger's way, he was still seated with his head down.

I looked forward as Tom began speaking. "The purpose of this workshop is to learn about lucid dreaming; to develop the ability to 'wake up' or become conscious in your dreams and know you are dreaming."

I thought it weird that Tom didn't address the new attendee. I wondered if he even noticed him. Just then I heard the door in the back of the room close and turned to see that the stranger was no longer in his seat. Wrong workshop, I gathered. No one else was distracted by this, so I took a few deep breaths and then refocused on Tom.

He began to share some general but interesting information about various aspects of lucid dreaming. "There are three common types of lucid dreams. The first is for fun and adventure. In this dream you can fly, go through walls, live out your sexual fantasies safely . . ." I looked over toward Alex who was taking copious notes. ". . . or do anything else you desire."

"The second type of lucid dream is for interpretation. Simply allow whatever is happening to continue to happen. Do not alter the dream, which, by the way, can be done with a simple snap of the fingers or clap of the hands. Just make every effort to be an observer, trying only to grasp the meaning in the dream's message.

"The third type of lucid dream is for receiving information. You can ask questions of any person in your dream." Now I was the one taking copious notes. Tom continued, "Because you're not dis-tracted by your physical senses, this state of mind allows you access to the part of you that knows the answers to all questions. I call this my Higher Coach."

This guy is pretty cool, I thought.

"There are many ways to have lucid dreams, and these days there are pills and tools and many more techniques than when I first started lucid dreaming about forty years ago. I tried a few of the newer ideas but found that the basics worked best for me. Get ready to take some important notes," he prepared the class, though everyone was already writing at that point.

"Throughout your day, think about lucid dreaming and the type of lucid dream you want to have. Repeat to yourself, as often as you can, 'Tonight I will have a lucid dream.' It may help to put a rubber band around your wrist as a visual reminder to repeat the saying. You may also try meditating on the center of your forehead where the sixth chakra, or third eye, is located. Tibetan tradition says this enhances the process of lucid dreaming. If after the first few nights you haven't had a lucid dream, set an alarm to wake up two hours earlier than normal, meditate, repeat the saying, and go back to sleep. You are then more likely to have a lucid dream.

"I highly recommend keeping a dream journal. As soon as you wake up, write down whatever insights you got from your dream and as much as you can remember. Also, in case you were wondering, everyone remembers lucid dreams, so if you've had trouble remembering your dreams, once you get good at this, that shouldn't be an issue." I nodded in appreciation of that comment.

Tom talked for a while more, mostly to share some history on the subject and then said, "I'll stop to see what questions you have."

Alex quickly shot his hand up. "Yes, Alex?" Tom inquired. I heard someone gasp.

"Yeah . . . how do I know what I'm experiencing is a dream?" Alex asked. I breathed a sigh of relief and was sure I heard a few other tension-reducing exhales as well.

"There are many signs in the dream world that will let you know you're dreaming. In your dreams, things tend to be distorted. A clock or watch may be moving backward or not working at all, or it may be blurry or have strange numbers on it. A car may be flying. Your hair might be a different color or style.

"I like to test myself while I'm awake—for example, I might try to lift a really heavy piece of furniture with one finger—which doesn't work when I'm awake but could in a dream. You can come up with your own tests and practice them while you're awake so you'll know the difference when you apply them in your dreams. I ultimately found that just looking at my watch was all I needed. If it worked right, I was awake. If not, I was dreaming. I found that works for most others, too.

"Another key to knowing if you're dreaming is to simply ask yourself 'Am I dreaming?' If you keep asking it during the day, you will find that you'll start asking it in your dreams, at which time you will be able to apply your test and know if you are having a lucid dream."

Another participant, Rachel, raised her hand, asking "How do we keep the lucid dream going? I've had a few of them, and every time I realize I'm dreaming, I just wake right up."

Tom patiently responded. "I always just spin around in my dream a couple of times, and that has kept me sleeping and lucid. Other people find that rubbing their hands together in the dream accomplishes the same thing. Other questions?" No hands went up.

"Let me say one more thing that I've noticed. When I feel any tension or stress in the dream, I usually wake right up or just lose dream awareness until I do actually wake up in the morning, so if you find yourself in a dream, try not to create situations that cause you stress."

I wrote that down but didn't think it was very important at the time. Tom wrapped up with some stories from his personal experiences, and there was some lively conversation, but I didn't participate in it or pay much attention. My mind was wandering and I was looking forward to getting to bed.

4

From the moment I got in a cab for the ride home until I passed out on my pillow, I recited two phrases: "I will have a lucid dream tonight," and "Am I dreaming?" For the latter, I looked at my watch to see if it was working properly.

I must have drifted off to sleep around midnight. Sometime in the middle of the night, I had a dream. During it, I remember asking myself if I was dreaming. At that moment, I looked at my watch, and it wasn't working. I remember thinking "Oh my God!" Tom told us that stress could halt the process. I guess that meant *good* stress, too, because I suspect my excitement caused me to lose lucidity. The next thing I experienced was my alarm clock going off at its usual time, 6:59 a.m. I always set it for that time because I felt it gave me a one-minute head start for the day. Usually it didn't matter, because I would just lazily lie in bed for another twenty to thirty minutes, but this time I bounced out of bed, excited beyond belief. Besides having my first lucid dream experience, I remembered it, which was in and of itself exciting enough.

I showered, dressed quickly, and then tried calling Larry to tell him about the workshop and the dream. His voicemail picked up, and I left a message; I'm not sure what I was thinking, as Larry's day as a teacher would have already begun. But I still had some time before I needed to be at my office, so I decided to honor my promise to Larry and contact my old therapist, Jean Carlson.

The last time I'd seen Jean was about two years earlier when I felt like I was periodically having some sort of anxiety attacks. Jean was not one to hold anything back and told me flat out that I was under too much stress and needed to start doing relaxation exercises or else. She also said there were some unresolved issues that I needed to work on, but I figured that was just shrink talk for "please keep paying me." I stopped working with her when she started pushing me to talk about my past. The anxiety did lessen, though, with the help of the relaxation techniques she taught me.

I still had her number in my phone and dialed her, knowing that unlike teachers, therapists aren't usually at the office that early. That way I could just leave a message, which I did. Since I just stopped going to sessions, I figured we didn't end on wonderful terms, and part of me hoped she wouldn't call back.

As I left my apartment building to head to the office, I saw my neighbor, Greg Allen, tinkering with his bike. About six feet tall, very fit, and always impeccably dressed, Greg was the consummate extrovert who could speak to anyone about anything. Intelligent and charming, he always seemed to have people around him. If there was a vote for most popular person in the building, he'd have won by a landslide.

"Hey, Greg. How are you?" I inquired.

"I'm fine. Hope things are well with you," he said and then returned his focus to his bike.

That quick interlude was typical of the way things were between us those days. Cool and cordial. I'd been in the building for about ten years, and Greg had been there even longer. At one time, we were pretty close friends, but over the last few years, other than a quick hello as we passed each other coming or going in the building, we'd not spent much time together. I wasn't sure what happened between us. I wanted to rekindle our friendship, but I avoided doing anything to make that happen, thinking that he wouldn't be as interested. I had decided to keep things the way they were rather than to force the issue or worse, find out that I was right and that he no longer wanted to be my friend.

When I got to work, the door to my office was blocked by a ladder. Nowell, the maintenance guy, was working on the ceiling tile above the door, and there was no way for me to get through.

I always thought Nowell to be an unusual, perhaps eccentric kind of a guy. I guessed he was in his late forties or early fifties, but I wasn't sure. He had a full head of meticulously kept short brown hair that showed just a hint of gray. He always wore the same clothes—a white tee shirt tucked into blue cargo pants fastened by a pair of red suspenders. In all my years working there, I didn't remember him ever wearing anything else, and I didn't think I'd ever had more of a conversation with him other than "Hey, Nowell" and "Hi, Mr. Billings."

"Hi, Mr. Billings."

"Hey, Nowell." Without another word, suspenders and all, he came down the ladder and moved it so I could get inside.

Just as I sat at my desk, my cell phone rang. I picked up and Larry jumped right in, "I have a prep period so I can talk for a few. So how was the workshop?"

"It was pretty cool. I learned a lot and then actually had a lucid dream last night! I was shocked."

"That's wild," he said. "Who'd have thought it could be that easy? What happened in the dream?"

"Oh, well, I just got a little excited and lost the awareness. The whole thing only lasted a second or two. But I remembered it, so apparently I do dream."

Larry laughed and then asked a couple of details about the process I learned. I told him it was a skill, like any other, and that I'd need to practice it to the point where I could be lucid for as long as I'd want. He sounded very interested and excited for me. Then he said something that brought the chill back into my body.

"Did you meet anyone interesting at the workshop?"

I told him about the sex-obsessed guy, Alex, and then I shared a few more observations about some of the other people there, as well as Tom, the presenter. I thought about what to say next, and then continued. "There was also someone else there. He came late. He wore all gray and . . ." I stopped right there, realizing that I didn't really know what else to say about the stranger. "It doesn't matter. You need to get back."

"Actually, I do. Thanks. Talk later," he said before disconnecting.

I asked Karine to come in to my office and then remembered the ladder, which was again blocking the door. I saw Nowell move the ladder for her and was surprised to see her give him a hug. I continued watching as the two of them had what seemed to be a lively conversation. I didn't know that Nowell was even capable of having a conversation. It was then that I realized Karine had a beautiful smile. I didn't recall ever seeing it before.

I didn't want to make more of a big deal out of the big deal, but it was huge, and since Damon had given me a not-too-subtle warning, I figured that we'd better land it or I could be in real trouble. Also, since there would be a very sizable bonus that came from securing the account, I wanted to make sure Karine knew just how important this deal was.

I watched as Nowell folded up the ladder and walked away, waving goodbye to Karine, who was no longer smiling when she entered my office. "Hi, Karine. Have a seat. I just wanted to talk with you about the Concord account again. What do you know about Eric Concord?" I asked.

A look of confusion passed over her face. "He's a big movie star, right? Has some sort of investment company, I think, but I'm not sure."

Did she just say she thinks *he's a big movie star?* I asked myself, somewhat incredulously. Eric was a twenty-plus-million-dollar-a-movie A-list star with more credits to his name than almost any other actor in Hollywood. How could she not know that? His group's real estate holdings were rumored to be in the billions. This was, by far, the largest potential account in the company's history, and Karine's answers didn't make me feel very comfortable. But I didn't recall her ever not closing a new account, so I decided that I'd have to trust her like I always did, even for this one. Other than actually going out and securing the account myself, the thought of which scared the crap out of me, I really had no other option, anyway.

"Okay, Karine, thanks. I know you'll be great. I'm just thinking about how important it is that we pull this off." Since it was really her and not me, I had a twinge when I said the word "we."

"Not to worry. I'll make sure Mr. Concord has a good experience," she said, without any expression.

I hesitated at her choice of words, wondering for a moment if the "sexretary" nickname was indeed earned. Putting that out of my mind, I smiled and said, "Great, Karine, I know you'll do a fine job."

"Will there be anything else?" she asked, flatly.

"Well, just wanted you to know that if we get this account there will be something in it for you," I said, without thinking about what that would be. "Thanks again," I said, as she popped out of the chair and exited.

* * *

After Karine walked out, I rolled my chair over to the window and stared outside. I stayed there for quite a while, swiveling the chair left and then right, never taking my eyes off the spot where I saw the beggar.

It had now been over a week since I'd seen the light, and I'd been looking for it every day since. Unfortunately, it hadn't reappeared and looking out the window did little to nothing for me now except offer me a break from doing, well, very little to nothing. I looked forward to going to sleep each night to try to dream again, but other than that, it hit me that nothing else in my life was changing. I was still unmotivated, discouraged, and feeling guilty about not doing the job I was supposed to be doing.

I left the office at the end of the day and thought about going to Las Puertas for dinner but instead decided to just make myself a turkey sandwich at home. When I got there, Greg was standing outside, this time talking to another neighbor. I said hello to them both but didn't hear a response from Greg.

* * *

The next couple of weeks were a little boring and, even though I was having a lucid dream almost nightly, none of them lasted more than a few seconds. I thought the practice would pay off, but the 6:59 morning alarm was now a constant reminder that I had failed again. I was getting frustrated, so I decided to review my workshop notes. I was glad I did, as I had completely forgotten about the "stay-lucid" technique that Tom had shared with us. I decided that in my next lucid dream, I would spin around a couple of times so I could remain lucid. I looked forward to something different happening that night.

And something different did happen that night. Something truly amazing.

5

I was at the beach. It was a very hot summer day, and there weren't any clouds in the bright blue sky. Umbrellas and beach chairs dotted the sand, and the ocean was crowded with kids splashing each other in delight as they bounced in the waves. As I stood on the boardwalk and watched people walk by me, I could feel the sun warming my body and smell the scent of the ocean air. I looked down the boardwalk and noticed a beautiful woman with long blond hair wearing a yellow bikini leaning against the rail that separated the boardwalk from the beach.

"Am I dreaming?" I asked. As had become my habit, I checked my watch, and it wasn't working. I thought I might wake up, since I had rarely made it past the point of checking my watch in previous dreams, so I quickly spun around two times. It worked! I was still lucid. My first inclination was to try to fly, so I ran down the boardwalk, past the blond-haired woman, and took off. It was a very poor attempt; I got a foot off the ground and traveled only a few yards before I fell to the boardwalk. It was a great feeling to fly and a not-so-great feeling to hit the hard boardwalk. I again sensed that I was about to wake up, so I got to my feet and spun around a few more times. Still sleeping and still lucid, I felt bruised but awesome, like a little boy who just got off a ride on the bumper cars.

I doubled back to the woman on the railing and stood behind her, feeling unsure about pursuing my next urge. Without looking at me, she reached her arms back, took hold of my hands, and then pulled them around her waist.

6:59.

"Wow!" I yelled out loud as I sat up in my bed. While Tom had told us what was possible in a lucid dream, I was amazed at what I had just felt and the fact that the dream lasted as long as it did. I was also amazed at its clarity and detail. I felt the heat of sun, the pain from the fall on the boardwalk, the smell of the ocean air, and the softness of the woman's body, all at least as real as anything I'd ever experienced.

* * *

As I did on many a Saturday morning, I texted Larry to see if he was up for a visit. When he replied that he was, I hailed a cab and headed over.

Larry and his family lived in a small, two-family home not far from Arthur Avenue, the "Little Italy" of the Bronx, where delicious pasta and cannoli were available on every block. I always stopped in at this great coffee shop on his corner to pick up two large coffees on my way to his house. It was an unusually warm day, and Larry was waiting on his awning-covered porch when I got there, pointing his finger at me as I handed him his coffee and immediately began recounting my dream from the night before. I left out the last part about how the woman had touched me. Though I trusted Larry implicitly, I sometimes tried to hold back details that were embarrassing—not because he would judge me, but only because when I verbalized those things, I would judge myself more than I normally did. Larry was a great man. I wasn't totally sure why he remained my friend.

"It was incredible," I said, excitedly.

"That's great! So, what did you ask?"

"What do you mean?" I asked.

"You said you wanted to get some answers, right?"

I had been so caught up in the experience of the lucid dream that I had forgotten why I decided to do it in the first place. "Uh, yeah, of course. Just figured I'd explore a bit before getting to that."

"Sounds good. Just remember not to get too caught up in things that aren't that important to you," he said, as if he was reading my mind. And even though I knew he was right, the prospect of what could happen with the dream woman was definitely exciting.

Moments later, Larry's daughter Paula walked out onto the porch with us. "Hi, Uncle Scott," she said. At seventeen, Paula was tall with long dark hair that was always tied in a ponytail. Perhaps because she was an only child, she was much more comfortable with adults than she was with her peers. Larry encouraged her to prepare for the future, so instead of socializing, she spent her time studying and practicing the cello.

"Hey, Paula. How are the college interviews going?" I asked.

"I had a great talk with an admissions guy from the Stonebridge School of Music, and I really think I'm going to get in!"

"Really? Well, you're certainly talented enough," I commented.

"Thanks. I applied for one of their scholarships, and I think I have a very good chance of getting that, too."

"That's great, Paula. You deserve it," I said and meant it. Ginette then came out and joined us. I've always liked Larry's wife, but I didn't think she liked me very much. There were so many things she could judge; I wouldn't blame her. Maybe she, too, wondered why Larry was friends with someone like me. Sometimes Larry, Paula, and I would go to the movies or do something enjoyable, but Ginette rarely, if ever, joined us.

"Come on, Paula," she said. "We'll be late for the interview. Oh, hi, Scott." I'd gotten used to Ginette over the nearly twenty years they've been married, so I wasn't really bothered by the lack of enthusiasm she showed when speaking to me.

"Hey, Ginette. Where are you guys headed off to?" When I asked that, Paula's head dropped a bit, Larry looked away from the three of us, and Ginette seemed annoyed by my question.

"We're going to LaGuardia Community College for Paula's interview," she said, rather sternly.

I didn't say a word, as the picture here was as clear as the dream from the night before. What I surmised was that Larry and Ginette didn't see eye to eye on the college thing. Perhaps he believed in Paula more than her mother did. Perhaps Ginette was just more cautious. That part wasn't as clear to me.

I watched as Ginette and Paula headed down the street. Larry stood and said "Feel free to hang out if you'd like, but I should probably grade some papers. Got any other plans today?"

My only real agenda item was going to sleep. "Not much. Just relaxing. By the way, I did contact that therapist, but she hasn't gotten back to me. Not sure she will. But I just wanted to let you know I did what I said I would do." Larry was like a life coach to me, always holding me accountable so I would do what I said I was going to do. I appreciated that about him, even if I complained to him about it on occasion.

"Good job, man. Proud of you. And thanks for the coffee," he said.

I decided to take the subway home. Just as I got there, Greg was coming out of the elevator in the front lobby. I was disturbed that he ignored me the other day, but wasn't sure if or how to bring it up. The idea of us not being that friendly anymore nagged at me, but the thought of him actually being upset with me pushed my "I'm not good enough" button, which made me very uncomfortable.

"Hey, Greg, how are you?"

"I'm good, Scott. What's new with you?" he said, pleasantly.

I felt a sudden burst of courage. "Not a lot, but I did want to ask if you were upset about anything. You know . . . like, did I do something wrong?"

He looked away from me, but I was sure I could detect a slight frown on his face. I was sorry I'd spoken up. He started talking without looking directly at me and fumbled with his keys as he spoke: "I wouldn't say you did anything wrong, but now that you bring it up, Scott, I thought we were friends, but frankly, I got tired of our friendship always having to be on your terms. So, I stopped reaching out—you know—to see if you would. And you didn't. And the more time went by, the more I realized you never actually showed an interest in being a friend at all."

His words were like a punch to my gut. I took a deep breath before replying, "I had no idea you were that upset, Greg. I didn't mean to disappoint you. I'm really sorry."

He took a deep breath as well but didn't respond.

"I can do better," I said, really wanting to believe it. "I can be a better friend."

He frowned again and remained silent.

"Please just think about it, okay?" I asked.

"Well, I'm planning a bike trip in the Catskills this summer with a few of my friends. Maybe you'd like to join us?"

"I'll think about that, Greg," I said, not wanting to close the door again, even if I knew there was no way I'd go. I hadn't ridden a bicycle since I was a kid and wasn't brave enough to try it again. "Maybe we can do something together, sooner?"

He thought for a moment. "I am having a party next Saturday night. You could stop by if you wanted to."

I was sure he was testing me. "Yeah, I'll come to the party. Thank you. I really appreciate you giving me another chance. Means a lot to me."

"Okay, then. If I don't run into you sooner, I'll see you next Saturday. Starts at eight and will go to eleven or so," he said as he turned toward his apartment.

I felt relieved and terrified at the same time. Socializing was hard enough for me, but going to a party was flat out daunting.

I walked into my place, and when I put my phone down on the kitchen table I noticed there was a voice mail. Apparently, Jean had called a couple of days earlier to let me know that the upcoming Thursday at 6 p.m. was available. I texted her a confirmation, then to get full credit, I texted Larry to let him know. "Good job!" he texted back. "Don't forget to ask her why you repel all decent women," he added, with a wink. I smirked but didn't respond.

Still somewhat rattled from the encounter with Greg, I spent the rest of the day in a bit of a funk, just watching the golf channel, playing chess on my iPad, and surfing YouTube videos. As evening fell, though, I began getting excited about my upcoming dream date with the blond woman. I didn't miss the irony that I was going to bed *before* sex, instead of the other way around.

* * *

"Am I dreaming?" I looked at my watch, and it confirmed that I was. However, this time the scene had dramatically changed. I was in my office and working at my desk when Karine announced that I had a visitor. "Who is it?" I asked.

"She said you know who she is." Funny thing was, assuming it was the girl from the beach, I really didn't know who she was.

"Send her in, please," I said, all the while knowing that I was dreaming and that some part of me was creating the dream as I went along. I still believed that I didn't know what would happen, though, and I didn't, especially when a different looking woman entered my office. This woman was a tall brunette. She wore a long, flowing, red dress that followed her every move.

"You changed your hair," I commented.

"You prefer blond?" she asked.

"Not really, I was just curious as to why you changed it and why we're here in my office," I replied.

"You prefer the beach?" she asked. I realized that both questions were not rhetorical and she was reminding me that I could snap my fingers and change the dream at any time. I'd definitely try that soon enough, but that wasn't the most important thing on my mind at that moment.

The woman walked past me and looked outside the window. It was dark outside, so I doubted if she could see anything. As she bent over and leaned on the windowsill, her dress hugged the curves of her body, showing off a voluptuous figure. She then turned to face me while slowly lowering herself to rest on the windowsill.

I sat in my chair and watched this gorgeous being as she looked back into my eyes with a wanting that I'd not seen before. She slowly and gracefully arose from the windowsill, walked toward me, then bent over to kiss me.

I didn't expect her lips to feel as soft, warm, and moist as they did. I was sure I'd wake up, which was happily not the case. She then stood again and, with a subtle motion, put a finger on each side of her dress straps and pushed them off, allowing the dress to fall to the ground in slow motion.

Just at that moment, I heard something outside my office door and turned my head to see Karine right outside, looking in at us.

"What the hell are you looking at!?" I yelled, startling myself with my reaction. My next thought was how loud my alarm clock seemed.

I was upset with myself for forgetting to turn off my alarm for a Sunday. I tried to fall back asleep, but it was not to be.

6

From the moment I woke up, all I could think of was getting through the day so I could get to sleep that night. To help burn off some frustration and energy, I got dressed and went for a run. I headed down the cross street over to Central Park and began running my usual route at an easy pace. In contrast to the brief warm spell of the day before, that day was cold and clear. As I ran, I admired the beautiful leaves that remained on the branches of the magnolia trees.

I was about 200 yards from the Bethesda Fountain near the lake in Central Park. I always loved looking at the statue in the middle, the magnificent Angel of the Waters, which supposedly blessed New York's water supply. The fountain offered seating around its perimeter for passersby who might not be bothered by an occasional misting from some windblown water. At that time of the year, few people took advantage of the resting spot.

However, one person was there, and I was pretty sure I'd seen him before. I stopped dead in my tracks when I got the confirming chill of recognition. It was the creepy stranger from the dream workshop, still wearing the same gray clothes and black baseball cap. My heart raced faster than it had when I was running, and I noticed a sweat covering my skin that had not been apparent before.

"Not that unusual," I said out loud, trying to avoid panicking, "I've run into people from other parts of my life while jogging in Central Park; it's a common place to be." My rationalization wasn't working, and I was deeply afraid. I gathered enough courage to take a closer look and began a slow walk toward him.

When I was about thirty feet away, I could see that he was still holding the same book that he was carrying when I saw him in the workshop. Just as in the workshop, his head was down. I then realized that since I recognized him, he could do the same with me, which was enough for me to turn around and begin running in the other direction, out of the park.

I felt like a loser for literally running away from my fears, but I wasn't so sure that confronting him was a safe thing to do.

When I got home, I jumped into the shower and stood there for several minutes with my back to the shower head, allowing the water to pulsate over my body. I then turned and put my hands on the wall and felt the water on top of my head. Finally, I forced myself to get out. Though I was still unnerved, I pretty much repeated my activities of the day before, after which a light dinner and a boring documentary allowed me to relax enough to settle into bed.

I closed my eyes, and next thing I knew, I found myself in my office again; watch not working.

"You have a visitor," Karine said, after which the entire dream from the night before was replayed nearly exactly, except that the woman, whose hair was blond again, was much shorter and several years younger than in the previous dreams.

Each of her enticing moves was similar, though, and as I expected, Karine looked in on us again. This time, I snapped my fingers and to my surprise and delight, the woman and I were at a campground inside of a tent, with no Karine in sight. I did hear people walking around the tent and was concerned about them looking in on us, but I was too engrossed in the heat of the moment to let that bother me.

And an amazing moment it was, as the two of us settled into a slow and passionately engaged rhythm. We made love for what seemed like hours, and the feeling of connection and oneness was unlike anything I'd ever experienced. I was indeed a happy camper.

When I woke up, I asked myself two questions: The first was, *Am I dreaming?* and the second, which made me laugh out loud, was, *Do I have a girlfriend?*

Over the next few nights, I lost count of the exact number of lucid dreams I had, but they were all spectacular. Besides acting out some fantasies, I did more flying and got pretty good at it. One time, I flew up into space and just watched as the moon orbited the earth and asteroids flew by me. In that dream, I saw something unusual—some sort of entranceway in space. I peered at it for a while, puzzled by what I saw. It was not quite a rectangular doorway and not circular, either; it was something in between. Looking from a distance through its glass-like opening, I saw that there were no stars on the other side and wondered if it was a black hole. Suddenly, I felt a strong pull to go through the entranceway, much like the pull I experienced toward the light outside my office window. As I moved closer, however, I woke up.

The entranceway to what I thought of as some sort of portal appeared in other dreams and in many other locations as well. Each time I approached it, I would lose lucidity. Even spinning around didn't work. I could see it, but could never get close enough to see what was on the other side. In one dream, I decided to ask the woman about the portal.

We were lying on the deck of a huge yacht, staring at the sky. I felt relaxed and peaceful and was very happy to have her right next to me. A few soft, white clouds moved overhead, and when they did, I could see the portal. "Can I ask you a question?"

"Of course," she replied.

I raised my arm to point to the sky and asked, "What is that?"

The answer I got came from my alarm clock and was not the one that I wanted to hear. I immediately felt irritable. Time to get back to the real world.

* * *

The waiting room was pretty much how I remembered it. Jean's diplomas and certificates of achievement were everywhere, mixed in with an occasional plant for balance.

"Good to see you, Scott," said Jean, in the professional way I remembered. "Come right in."

I sat in the same comfortable reclining chair that I'd used previously.

"Why don't you begin by telling me what brought you back here today?"

I felt like I needed to be careful with Jean. I knew she was a great therapist and I did believe in the value of therapy, but I didn't want her to judge me. I hated being judged by anyone, especially someone in a position of authority.

"I'm not sure where to start. I've been stressed out at work and, at the same time, pretty much disengaged. Nothing else much is interesting enough to share, except that I can report that I've been sleeping very well." I hoped she didn't notice the suppressed chuckle.

"I see," she said. "From what I remember and have in my notes, two years ago you said something similar about your job. Not much seems to have changed there for you. Do you think that still being there might be the main cause of your stress right now, or might there be something else?"

"Could be the job, I guess. I really don't enjoy what I do anymore, but I suppose there's also something else that's been bothering me. Maybe it's a midlife crisis or something, but I really don't feel any purpose when I'm awake." After I said that, I immediately regretted doing so.

"I'm sorry, did you say, 'when you're awake'?" she asked, leaning forward in her chair.

"Uh, yeah . . . I mean . . . like I said, I've been sleeping well and having some interesting dreams," I said, without giving her any indication that I wanted to talk about that.

"I see," she said and jotted a few things on her notepad. "You're trying to tell me that you like your dream life better than your real life?"

"I . . . didn't think of it that way, but if I have to be honest . . ." I paused to offer her the opportunity to say something, which she didn't. "I think maybe I do," I continued.

"Thanks for being honest with me. I appreciate that, because it makes our time together more worthwhile. What do you find so interesting about your dreams?" she asked. I couldn't read her intention in asking.

"I just think there are a lot of messages for me in them. Things I can learn about myself." As I said that, I thought how ridiculous my statement was, given the nature of the dreams to that point. I tried turning the tables. "What do you think about the dream world?" I blurted out, again, immediately regretting the question.

"If I might, perhaps the question should be what do I think about *your* dream world. But let's come back to that. First, let me ask you, how have your romantic relationships been?"

"I did meet someone, but I don't think it'll be a long-term thing."

"What's her name?"

Amazingly, it was the first time I realized that I didn't know the name of the dream woman. I knew I had to come up with something quickly. "Skye. Her name is Skye." That was the last thing I remembered seeing while lying on the yacht in my previous dream, and I figured it was as good a name as any other.

She was silent for a few minutes, sat back in her chair, looked at her notes, then at me, and then back at her notes.

"Can I tell you what I think is going on here?" she asked, but didn't wait for a reply. "I apologize in advance if what I'm about to say is hard to hear, but you know how much I care about you and that I believe a direct approach is the best." I braced myself.

"First, the stress you feel is probably not so much job related as it is due to your overall dissatisfaction with your life. You mentioned feeling purposeless, which could explain your dream fascination, as that could be your real-world escape. But more importantly, I'm getting the feeling that your self-image is the culprit here. I believe you actually continue to re-create your life as a self-fulfilling prophecy, or more accurately, a self-defeating one. This is evidenced by your history of superficial relationships and staying at a job you say you don't enjoy." She paused. I didn't say a word.

"I believe you stay at your job because you feel you don't deserve to be happy. Your relationships suffer as well, because if you don't love or even like yourself, why would you expect to find someone else who does?

"I think all of this is from a very old wound that will not be healed until you are willing to face it. This new dream fascination you've mentioned is disturbing, because instead of dealing with the past issues that are holding you back, you went in a completely different direction—disassociating from the real world and creating an alternate reality."

She paused again. I just sat there.

"I hope that didn't sound too bleak, because I don't see it that way. If you're willing to take therapy seriously this time, I believe we can work through this. I also believe that a part of you knows that, and that's why you reached out to me again. But taking it seriously will require you to face some old pain, which is something you've avoided in the past. And there's one more thing and please listen to me . . ." She leaned forward for the next part and pointed her pen at me for a sterner warning. "You need to let the dream thing go. It is dangerous and can only lead to a more severe disassociation from reality.

"Tell me what you're thinking, Scott."

I didn't make eye contact as I thought everything through. "Well, I'm open-minded enough to consider some of what you said as possible, but I don't agree that the dreams might harm me. I have a strong feeling about their value to me."

"It might help if I gave you a little education about dreams. The main purpose of dreaming is to help us process and release recent emotional experiences in order to lessen anxiety. Dreams also allow the brain to store short-term memories so as not to keep the mind too active with a lot of extraneous thoughts. So that's the truth, Scott. Please don't make more of them than what they are."

"You don't know the truth, so I would appreciate it if you didn't say you did!" I declared, surprising myself more than her, I suspected.

She raised her eyebrows. "I don't think I've ever heard you stand up for what you believed in before. How are you feeling about that?"

"I feel like maybe it was a mistake to come back here."

"I understand. Know that I don't think it was a mistake at all. I think it was very wise on your part. Please relax, and if it's okay with you, how about taking a deep breath?" she requested, and I complied.

"Scott, I do know you to be open-minded. I'd like to help you relax a little more. Like we used to do. Then, if you're willing and open, I'd like to ask you a few questions and perhaps do a short regression to see if we can find something to help you. Will that be okay?"

I nodded, but had I truly understood what she was asking of me, I would have declined.

I settled deeper into the reclining chair while she turned on some meditation music. She then guided me to relax different body parts. We had done that exercise numerous times before, so I was able to relax fairly quickly.

"Okay, Scott. Staying relaxed and open-minded as you are, I want you to now count backward in your mind, repeating after me as we descend from ten to one. Ten (ten), nine (nine), eight (eight) . . ."

She reached "one," then I didn't hear anything else for a while until I heard her ask me if it was okay to go back and think about my fondest memory as a child.

"Yes, that's okay," I said in a soft intonation, "but I can't think of anything."

"Take your time," she said, comforting me.

"I . . . I am on vacation in upstate New York with my dad," I finally said.

"That's great. Tell me how you're enjoying it."

"My dad and I are alone on a fishing and camping trip. It's a lot of fun. I love going fishing with my dad." I felt myself smile but didn't feel in control of doing that.

"And now, equally relaxed and without feeling any emotion, tell me about your least favorite memory as a child," she said.

I started to twitch a little and felt an overwhelming sense of fear.

"Don't worry about what happened for now," she said in a reassuring tone. "Just tell me *when* it happened."

"I don't know," I mumbled.

"Was it around five years old?"

"Earlier," I said but had no idea why I said it.

"Four years old?"

"Earlier," I repeated.

"Three years old?"

"Around then, yes," I said, quietly but confidently, still not having any idea how I knew that information.

"So, what happened then, when you were around three years old?"

"My parents are fighting. There is a lot of screaming, and my father is doing most of it. They don't know I can see and hear them clearly."

"What else is happening?" she asked. I then felt a wave of terror run through me that shot me up in my chair. I breathed heavily and opened my eyes.

"I don't want to do this anymore," I said anxiously.

"You don't have to. You did great. We can stop here. I think, a little at a time, we can help you process what happened all those years ago. Can you come back at the same time next week?" she asked.

"Yeah, okay," I said, figuring I'd cancel before the appointment.

7

"Well, that was pretty deep. Are you going to keep your appointment?" Larry asked after I filled him in what was going on in my dreams and in my "real" life, ending with the therapy session.

"I don't think so, but I'm not sure. I have a week to think about it," I said as I sipped a Las Puertas piña colada.

"Well, let me know if you'd like my opinion," he said.

"I think you just gave it to me!" I laughed. Larry smiled. "I really *would* like your opinion about a couple of things, though. First, what do I do about the stalker?"

"We don't know he's a stalker. You only saw him twice, and neither time did he try to engage you. Could just be a coincidence. I don't know that there's too much you can do at this point, anyway. That said, what would make you more comfortable?"

"I don't know, man. I can't avoid a guy that might be following me. I could confront him, I guess. Or, maybe you could . . ." I suggested, only half kidding.

"Want me to hit him for you?" he joked.

"Ouch," I said, still smiling. "You're right. Here's the deal. If he shows up again, I'll just ask him what he wants, and if I think I'm in danger, I'll just run. I'm sure he wouldn't be able to catch me."

"Plan," he said. "What else?"

Before I could answer, the waitress brought our dinners. I asked for another piña colada. I sipped the rest of the first drink and handed the empty glass to her, saying, "Thank you, ma'am" as she carried it away. I then continued with Larry.

"The portal. This is baffling. Why do you think I can't get in? It's a dream, right? I'm in control, no?"

"Maybe something's stopping you? Stress, perhaps? Didn't you say that you learned something like that in your dream workshop?"

That was a good question, and I figured it was time to share some of my dream encounters with the woman. I started from when I first met her on the boardwalk. Without sharing all the intimate details, I finished with the question I asked her while lying on the boat, looking at the portal.

"Holy crap!" he said. "You did meet your dream woman, I guess. Sounds like a really cool experience." Suddenly, he looked very concerned. "But now I have a question: What exactly are you doing?"

"What do you mean?" I responded.

"Oh, I don't know. My friend Scott thought he might have seen God and maybe even felt heaven. That guy told me that he would do anything to have that experience again and answer some of life's most probing questions in his dreams. So what has he learned?" he asked, teasingly.

"Shit," I said too loudly as the waitress was returning with my drink. She just smiled, but one of the other two customers in the restaurant gave me a dirty look. "Sorry," I said to the gentleman, and he got back to his meal. I turned back to Larry. "Sorry, Lar. What I meant to say was f*ing shit," I whispered.

Larry grinned, but then looked serious. "So, really, what are you doing, Scottie?" he asked again.

"I don't know," I said, lowering my gaze to the steam coming off my plate.

"You know what? I don't know, either!" he said, while doing the Larry belly laugh. "Honestly, and I could be way out of my league here, so take it with a grain of salt, but I agree with you that you need to explore these dreams more deeply."

"Thanks. I appreciate your support," I said. We then finished our meals, including my third piña colada, without talking about anything too deep. That was a good thing, since I wouldn't have been able to concentrate. I was too distracted thinking about what he said while asking myself over and over again if I was dreaming.

* * *

My alarm went off the next morning at 6:59. No lucid dream at all. Between that, the therapy session, and possibly too many drinks, I just didn't feel great. I called Karine and told her I wouldn't be in. I moped around the house for most of the day until a loud bang on the door startled me.

"Larry, what are you doing here? Don't you have a class?"

"School's over for the day. Do you even know what time it is?" he asked. I didn't. "I called you at work and they said you were out for the day. Then I called your cell and you didn't answer. I figured I'd better get over here to see if you were okay."

"Sorry. I'm fine, I just felt out of it and decided to hang home."

"Well . . ." he looked me over. "Okay. Anyway, I've been thinking about what you told me about the portals in your dreams. I have an idea about how to get in."

"Really? What?" I asked, feeling the first sign of enthusiasm that day. Larry is usually a cool character who wasn't in a rush about anything. This time, however, he excitedly jumped right in.

"I couldn't stop thinking about what you told me, and I know I shouldn't have to say this, but I'm going to give you an idea, not a fact." I nodded, and Larry continued. "When you were telling me about your dream woman, I got the impression you weren't totally comfortable sharing all the details. I think that's significant. Your discomfort makes me think that you're not being true to yourself and you're feeling guilty about that. I think going through the portal is the next step you need to take, but the guilt you feel needs to be dealt with before you will be able to move forward."

I thought about what he said. "Yeah, could be. I mean, I don't feel good about what I'm doing in those dreams. I don't even know the name of the woman I keep dreaming about. Maybe I need to pass some kind of test or elevate myself to a level that allows me to move forward? That makes sense."

"If I can be completely honest with you," Larry continued, "I'll tell you that whether it's your dream or waking life, you probably do need to make some changes."

"Yeah. You're right. I'll do something different. Maybe even tonight. You really think that's the key to getting through the portal?"

"Yeah, I think the portal is the future. I think that in your dreams, you're acting like a teenager. I mean, you're in the past. So, in order to get to the future, you need to let go of the past."

I heard him but didn't answer at first. "So, living in the past . . ." I stopped there and dove back into deep contemplation.

I was barely coherent as I heard myself ask if he wanted to get something to eat before he headed out, but he said he needed to get home quickly as the girls were expecting him for a family meeting about Paula's college options.

8

Before bed, I thought about what I might do differently in my next dream. Remembering Larry's remark about acting like a teenager, I set an intention to focus more on what really mattered to me.

That night, I found myself in the stands at an equestrian event, watching the competition. There was a large crowd cheering on the riders. One of the horsewomen rode past me, then doubled back and pulled up in front of me. She was wearing cream-colored jodhpurs with light brown leather patches on the inside of her thighs, ending at her high leather boots. Woven into her shirt were gold threads that shimmered as the light hit them, reflecting the highlights in her hair.

Something about her energy was different this time, and I wondered if my new intention for the dream was the cause of that. She dismounted and made her way up to sit next to me in the bleachers. We were now the only ones at the arena; even her horse was gone. I reached for her hand and she gave it to me freely.

"I want to apologize for something," I said.

"It's Lucena, and there's nothing to apologize for," was her quick reply.

"Lucena? As in lucid?" I asked

"You could say that," she said with a giggle.

"How do you know what I was apologizing for?"

"We are one, Scott. I thought you'd have figured that out."

"You're me?" I asked.

"In a sense. Probably best to think of me as a reminder—*your* reminder. I am here to remind you that the answers you seek are already within you, waiting to be revealed. All you need to do to access them is to 're-mind,' or reconnect with the part of you that knows.

"I have reached out to remind you in many ways. You've seen me in books you've read, in songs you've heard on the radio, in workshops, while you were in nature, and mostly, in silence. I'm also, as you now know, within your dreams. I've been there all along. There are other reminders waiting for you. You will meet them on your journey."

Her words reminded me of my conversation with the beggar: *There are always signs, everywhere, and it's your choice whether or not to see them.*

"So you're not a real woman?" I felt weird asking that of someone in my dream, but the question felt right to me.

"I'm as real as you are," she said with a smile and then continued. "I know you have a lot of questions and want answers. I could give you a lot of those answers, but learning something from someone and experiencing it firsthand are two very different things. That said, go ahead and ask your questions, and I'll answer as best I can."

I felt like a genie had just given me a bottle and told me I had three wishes. I didn't want to waste one with a stupid question, so I gave it some thought before I spoke. "My first question is, where am I moving forward to?"

"You are moving into a deeper state of awareness, a deeper awareness of reality. For now, think of your reality as the world you see through the filters you have developed over your lifetime. When we experience something, we create a belief about it. That belief filters our view of everything that happens thereafter. The deeper your state of awareness, the more likely the information you receive and translate will be unfiltered. You will develop a sense of knowing the difference between your reality and *the* reality. That will not happen immediately; you will have to have faith that it will come later in your journey.

"That journey will take you to people, places, and things that, until now, you would not have understood. And you are not really moving 'forward,' at least not the way you think of it, but you will understand that later on, as well."

I was concerned about asking the next question, as it had caused me to lose lucidity when I previously asked it, but I tried again. "What was that portal that I asked you about before?"

"You mean this?" she asked and pointed to the sky. I looked up to see a cloud move and the portal reveal itself. It then dropped from above to ground level. It was spectacular. I'd never seen anything quite like it. It was enormous, perhaps fifteen feet wide and tall, with a border built of some type of stone, perhaps granite. It hovered about three inches above the ground, but had no propulsion or other means to do so. In the center of the stone frame was something that resembled a piece of glass, but it also looked fluid, as if I could put my hand right through it. I was about to ask Lucena if I could try doing that, but just then another identical portal came into my line of sight and took its place next to the first one. Then, one by one, three more appeared. All of them were dark except for a slight glow that emanated from the granite-like border of the first one.

"I have been waiting for you to ask about this world. These are the windows to your soul, Scott. Yes, you can think of them as portals, that is, they allow you to see into, and then move through to, a deeper level of reality. We create these as a symbol of transition."

"We?" I asked.

"We, or I, or you. Depends on what you prefer. Those words all refer to the same thing." She looked my way. "Hope I didn't lose you."

She had, but I let it go. "When I first saw one, I thought it might have been a black hole," I stated.

"In a sense, that would be accurate, for within them time and space are irrelevant. You can be anywhere and at any time, past, present, or future, so to speak."

"I guess my next question is why. Why would I want to go into them? I mean, what is the real purpose of all this, anyway? Of course I am looking for answers, but most of all, I want what I felt when I met the beggar."

"The beggar?" She laughed. "Didn't get that one either, did you? Why do you suppose he begged for you to give him money?"

"I . . . don't know. When I asked him, he said it was his purpose. Wait, he did say that he was doing it for me. I really don't know why."

"Sure, you do. You already have the answers, Scott; you just need to remember. Let me remind you that you were feeling powerless in your life. By getting you to give him money, he allowed you to feel powerful, even for just a second."

I thought back to when I offered the beggar the ten-dollar bill. I did feel powerful—believing that I had the power to help him—and though I wasn't particularly proud of it, I realized I also felt somewhat superior to him.

"The purpose of this journey is to find yourself again . . . to remember the truth about who you are and why you are here. That is what you want. Doing so will also help you remember your power. The beggar, as you call him, started the process. It's now up to you to continue it. It may not be easy, but if you make it through all the portals, you will reach enlightenment, that is, the remembrance of the truth."

"What do you mean *if* I make it through?"

"You might decide that this is not your desired journey. Many others have said they wanted to know the truth, but what they really wanted was whatever they could find that agreed with what they already believed was the truth."

"Okay. I'm with you. So how do I get inside?"

"You can see that the first one is already starting to open because its light is beginning to shine. That opening occurred when you let go of your basic human desires and sought something deeper and more meaningful to you. Each portal is a deep part of you that is available to explore. You have the potential to enter them all, but you do not yet have the capacity, meaning the right frame of mind, or the keys to get in."

"How do I get those?" I asked.

"You will recognize when a key is given to you. As far as the frame of mind, you need to be curious, which is the state of having an inquisitive, child-like fascination, open-minded, so when you find the truth, you will be ready to let go of what you currently believe, and optimistic that you will find what you are looking for. You can remember it by the acronym 'COO'—curiosity, open-mindedness, optimism. Put them together and they lead to another 'O,' which is opportunity. You have an amazing opportunity available to you, and in order to experience it, you will need to demonstrate the COO to prove you are ready."

"Prove I'm ready to whom?"

"To yourself, of course. Only to you."

"I think I'm ready. Yes, I'm going to make it through all of them, Lucena."

"From your mouth to God's ears." She laughed almost as hard as Larry did during one of his belly laughs. I laughed as well, but had no clue what was funny. "Go, Scott. Enjoy the journey."

"Wait, can I ask another question?"

She thought about it for a moment before nodding in agreement. I wondered if she already knew what I was going to ask and if she was deliberating whether to answer me.

"This is a little embarrassing, but I would like to understand what possessed me to act like I did with you. I'm asking because . . . I'm not sure what that says about me."

"The primal brain seeks pleasure and controls your innate desires. What that says about you is that you are human. However, as important as sex might be for procreation and as much fun as it may be, it isn't related to that which you now seek."

I took a deep breath and asked "Is it ridiculous to have feelings for you? I mean, this is all a dream, right?"

"Like I said, I'm as real as you are, and no, it's not ridiculous. I love you, too."

Dream or not, it felt wonderful when she said that, and even before she did, I knew that I deeply loved this woman. I then asked if she could come with me.

"This journey ends now for me and continues for you, but don't worry; if you make it through all the portals, you will uncover the truth, and I will be there." She blew me a kiss before I woke up.

9

An early winter storm greeted me on Saturday morning by rapping its strong fingers on my bedroom window. I ignored it, once again finding myself distracted by the thought of what to do to fill the time between then and when I was able to go to sleep that night. I thought about going to a movie, but decided to do something a little more productive. I spent a couple of hours writing down some of my new insights and questions, did some stretching and pushups, and ended up doing two long-put-off projects, cleaning out a couple of cabinets and organizing my files. *Out with the old and making room for the new,* I thought to myself.

Before bed, I took out the garbage and saw Greg walking someone out of the lobby, apparently saying goodbye. I said hello to him, but he didn't respond. At that moment, I realized I had missed his party. Dejected and totally upset with myself, the thought *so much for turning over a new leaf* popped into my head. I even felt a little sick to my stomach, wondering if this was the final nail in the coffin for our friendship.

"I'm so sorry, Greg. I was preoccupied with something and completely forgot about your party. I really did mean to come. Really. I'm so sorry."

He turned toward me and I knew immediately that he was very upset. "You forgot about it? But if you had remembered, would you have come?"

I just stood there, not knowing what to say.

"Look, it's okay. Really. I should have known better than to actually think you would show up. Take care," he said as he walked back into his place.

I felt even worse. I really wanted to show him, and more so myself, that I could change. I thought about what Jean had said, and wondered if I actually could. Maybe I was kidding myself that cleaning and journaling meant that I was on a new path. Maybe a part of me missed the party on purpose. I just didn't know.

I had no real idea if it was the case, but a deepening queasiness told me that I had blown my chance for getting into the portal that night. That evening, my feeling was confirmed. During my dream, I stood before the five portals with the first one remaining only slightly lit. I couldn't tell if it had darkened a little after my encounter with Greg, but I wouldn't have been surprised if it had.

Thursday came, but I was in no mood to have another therapy session, so I left a message that I was ill and that I'd reschedule when I was feeling better. I figured Jean might charge me for the session, as I was within her twenty-four-hour cancellation policy, but I didn't care.

Over the next two weeks I considered apologizing to Greg again and wondered if it was my conflict with him that had caused my dream quest to stall, which it had. I saw the portals in every dream, but nothing about them changed. A few times I tried to put my hand in the first one, but it wouldn't go through, feeling more like glass than liquid. I did see Greg a few times in passing, but I couldn't get myself to say anything other than "Hey," after which he just nodded.

* * *

It was Wednesday, the day before the big Concord meeting. I hadn't spoken to Damon in quite a while. At one point late in the day, I saw him talking to Karine. He looked my way and then turned his attention back to Karine. I figured they were talking about me, and perhaps the Concord deal. Seemed like we were all in a holding pattern. Holding our breath, perhaps.

There had been no sign of the stranger in the black cap, so at least that was a good thing, but it had now been close to three full weeks since I'd seen Lucena. Between that, the job, and the Greg situation, I was feeling quite sorry for myself. I didn't even have enough energy or desire to look out the window. My pity party was interrupted by Karine, who burst into my office and closed the door behind her.

"Scott, we need to talk."

"What's going on?"

"I've always liked you. Unlike the other people here, you never disrespected me. So, I want to be completely honest with you now."

This was definitely not the same person I thought I knew all these years. Karine was sharp, powerful, and direct. I had to do a watch check to make sure I wasn't dreaming.

"I've been seriously contemplating a lot of things, and I'm going to lay it all on the line here. If I don't get the Eric Concord account, you're gone. And if I do get it, you're still gone."

"What?! How do you know that?"

"Damon basically told me so. He probably didn't even realize that I understood what he was saying. He told me to do whatever I could to get the account. I know what he meant. It made me sick to my stomach, and that's why I'm here. I'm done with this shit."

"I'm sorry about Damon. He's . . ."

"Forget it. It's all part of the game. I'm just done playing it by everyone else's rules. Listen, I work my butt off here. You have no idea. And I'm not complaining about the pay, which is actually pretty generous."

As soon as she said that, I felt guilty, because I knew she was compensated well, but not well enough for the work she really did. I looked at the pearl bracelet I'd given her, which I somehow thought would make up for that inequity, but seeing it just made me feel even more guilty.

"Listen, Karine, I do appreciate you and all you do for us. I said that if we got this account that there would be something in it for you . . ." She didn't let me finish.

"I don't think you understand. I am not going to land that account. You are."

I froze as a wave of panic shot through me. I tried to talk but felt a huge sickening lump in my throat that blocked the words. It took several deep breaths to calm me down enough to speak.

"Wh . . . what do you mean, Karine? I can't close that deal. I . . . I . . ."

"Stop it. That's just bullshit. You're better at this than anyone else I know. That's how I got so good at it. You taught me. You don't even see it. You're a brilliant strategist, and you're also very good at connecting with people when you want to."

I hesitated and looked at the floor as I spoke. "So, since you're being so honest here, I will be, too, and tell you that I really don't know if I can pull this off. I don't believe I can. And if I'm really going to be honest . . ." I looked up at her to continue. "I don't have what you have."

"You mean my body? Well . . . listen, I know some people think I sleep with the clients. I'm the 'sexretary,' after all."

"Oh, Karine . . . how . . ."

"Puh-lease!" she said emphatically. "You think I don't know what goes on here? I do. I basically run this whole place, Scott. I know every detail of this business, and one of those is that if you don't meet with Concord yourself, you can kiss this job goodbye."

As I considered Karine's words, I came to the conclusion that even though I'd complained a lot about the job, I really wasn't prepared to leave it at that point for many reasons, including financial ones. That realization must have prompted an insight, because it suddenly came to me that doing this might somehow be related to me being able to get into the portal. Maybe the COO I needed was to take action in spite of my fears.

"Karine, I'm not even sure I'd know where to start," I said, and then took a deep breath, "but I guess I could try."

"You do know where to start," she stated firmly. "How do you think I land all the accounts I do?"

"I . . . don't know."

"Of course you don't. You never asked. And that's fine. If I were in your shoes, I wouldn't know what to think, either. I do a ton of research on every single client, including looking into their hobbies, likes and dislikes, special interests, their families, their history, and anything else that will help me understand who they are and allow me to make a connection with them. Start there, Scott. You know how. I'm sure you don't remember teaching me how to do that, but you did. And you know what else? I always genuinely try to make each potential client I meet with a friend for life, regardless of whether I get their account, so think about that, too."

She then took out a file and dropped it on my desk. It landed with a bang that knocked some pens around. It said Eric Concord on it and was the size of an old encyclopedia.

"I'm really sorry, Karine. I had no idea. I'm very embarrassed around the assumptions I've made about you. I've learned an important lesson."

"Still having a truth truce, Scott?"

"Of course," I said.

"So right now, you're humble, open, honest, and even vulnerable. All those things are real, and they are very attractive. Embrace them and use them with Concord. I know you can do this. I have faith in you and I trust you. And besides, if you don't get the account, we're both gone, as Damon will freak out that I passed the meeting on to you."

I wasn't sure why, but I started to feel more confident and powerful. "You're right, Karine. About everything. But I don't really understand why you're doing this."

"I'm tired of the charade," she said with a stern frown. "It's so draining trying to be the image of what others want me to be. I'm acting here. I acted with you just the other day, playing dumb about how much I knew about Eric Concord. Did you really think that I didn't know who he was?" I looked at her sheepishly, remembering how concerned I'd been during that conversation. Karine went on without waiting for a reply. "I even pretend that I don't know how to type very well. I dress the part just to keep up the charade. I believed that they wouldn't give me the chances they have if they thought I was a threat to them. That if they knew the truth, they'd be jealous or intimidated, and I'd have a whole new set of challenges to deal with. But enough is enough. Like I said, I won't do it anymore."

"So, you're willing to risk your job? For me?"

"For you, and for me, too. Do you ever dream, Scott?"

"Uh, yeah, I can say that I do."

"I've been having a bad one for a long time and it haunts me. In it, I'm at my own funeral, and the room is filled with men. Someone asks, 'Does anyone have anything they'd like to say about Karine?' and they all snicker and no one comes up to speak. But I also have another dream. A powerful one. One I think about all the time. In that dream, I'm always completely myself, and I make a difference in the world, every day. It's time, Scott, for me to live that dream. I don't really care if I stay here or not. Either way, I'll be fine."

"Thank you, Karine. For the truth, for your trust in me, for everything. Thanks for never letting go of your real dream. I can do this. Just tell me how I can repay you for everything you've done for me."

"Well, I have a list! It's in another book, just about that size," she pointed to the Concord file, smiling. "Seriously, I will ask one thing of you, regardless of whether you get the account. Take Nowell out to dinner. I'm his only friend here, and he could use another one."

"That's it?"

"Well, one more thing, actually. Wear a nice buttoned-down blue shirt tomorrow."

"Really? Why?"

She again pointed to the Concord file. "It's all in there. You'll need to start reading now and probably pull an all-nighter to get ready."

I thought about Lucena's comment about having access to all information, past, present, and future. I felt my head nod and I said something that I would always remember as one of the most astonishing things I ever heard myself say. "Thanks, but I won't need the file."

"Scott, there's months of research in there."

"You said you trusted me. Well, trust me," I said.

* * *

That night, I saw the portals and although the first one seemed brighter than before, I didn't even try to get inside. Instead, I snapped my fingers and I was in front of a library. There was a statue of Rodin's *The Thinker* on one side of the entrance and a large marble globe on the other.

I entered and noticed there were no books, just an average-sized computer screen with no apparent processing unit. The screen was across the room, and I extended my arms forward and flew over to it.

I touched the screen, and like a giant iPad, a keyboard appeared on it. I typed in Eric Concord and saw his picture. When I touched it, I was transported to his early years, in what I figured was about the fourth grade. His teacher, Mrs. Kretzer, was asking the class what they wanted to be when they grew up. Eric's hand was the first to shoot into the air.

"A big movie star!" he shouted, with his hand still raised. The rest of the class laughed, even Mrs. Kretzer.

"That's exciting, Eric, but perhaps something a little more practical should be considered."

"Nope! That's what I'll be," he said and put his hand down. I imagined there wasn't a person in that classroom who could have wiped the smile from his assured face.

The scene then changed, and I witnessed him as a teenager in a car with a girl. They were parked near a beach at the Jersey shore looking out at the ocean on a beautiful and cloudless evening. He wore a blue shirt, which I somehow knew was his favorite piece of clothing. His arm was around the girl, and they kissed a few times.

"I'm so sorry, Grace. I just know that if I don't pursue my dream that my life will be wasted."

With tears in her eyes, she asked, "But why California, Eric? Why not just go to New York for acting?"

He explained that the opportunities on the West Coast were more advantageous for him and that leaving her was one of the hardest things he would ever have to do.

For the remainder of the dream, I watched Eric go through acting school, get rejected at multiple auditions, and land a small nonspeaking role in an independent film. I watched that movie from a theater, seated next to a man who had a small flashlight and was writing notes. The man was an agent, and I later saw the two of them at a Yankees game, toasting with a beer in celebration of Eric landing a leading role in an adventure movie.

The alarm woke me, and I wondered if I had dreamt the entire night. Regardless, I was ready.

* * *

I came to the office wearing a blue buttoned-down shirt. I was carrying a paper bag, which held a special something that I hoped would get a reaction out of Karine, who winked at me as I passed her desk and followed me into my office with a box in her hand. It had a bow on it.

"You look pretty good, but something's missing." She handed me the box. While I opened it, she said, "This is a reminder that the key to success starts with you getting out of your comfort zone." It was a thin polka-dotted tie that matched the blue shirt. "Tie it, you'll like it," she said with a smile.

"Everyone's a comedian," I replied. I went to the restroom to put the tie on and then looked in the mirror. "Ghastly!" I said. Karine was still in my office when I returned. I reached into the bag I brought and pulled out a Yankees hat. "How about this?" I said, excitedly.

"Nice touch with the hat! You *did* do your homework, and since I know you're a Mets fan, I'm even more impressed that you're willing to wear that. Oh, and nice tie."

"Well . . . I hate it," I said.

"No, you don't," she replied. She was right; even though I believed it was out of character for me, I actually loved it.

"I'm ready, Karine."

She looked me in the eyes and nodded. "I believe you are."

* * *

About an hour later, Karine knocked on my office door and walked in, accompanied by an extremely good-looking man in his mid-thirties, wearing a pair of chinos, Nike sneakers, a Mets hat that covered much of his blondish hair, a buttoned-down mauve shirt, and a thin polka-dotted tie. Mauve was my favorite color. *Oh my God, Karine!* I thought.

Karine made a quick introduction and left. Eric took off his sunglasses, looked at my tie, and said, "She got to you, too, huh, and I guess you're a Mets fan?" We shared a very comfortable laugh. "You know, you have one amazing colleague. Although I'm not so sure of her fashion sense."

Eric and I talked for more than three hours. I remembered what Karine had said and, early in the conversation, decided that I wasn't going to concern myself about getting the account. Instead, I'd present myself authentically and humbly, with the goal of helping him in any way I could.

Eric told me of his and his partners' real estate holdings, which he confirmed were valued in the billions. He also owned a number of restaurants on both coasts. I was shocked to learn that he lived in an average-sized home just outside the city, drove a five-year-old car, and besides going on vacation from time to time, spent very little money on himself. Instead, he used his money to help out his family, and he donated to several charities.

As I listened to his story, I could see he was a genuine, honest, and kind person. I shared a lot about me, as well, including the fact that I had not met with any new clients for more than five years, and that Karine "encouraged" me to make an exception in his case. I felt honored to have had that time with him and let him know that.

"Well, thank you," he said. "You have to believe me when I say it's my honor. Seriously. Karine told me so much about you. How great you are at what you do, how you truly care about people, and how honest you are. Except for your taste in baseball teams, I think you're a good guy."

My self-doubts rose right to the surface, and I cringed as he spoke those words. Still, a small part of me wondered if any part of what he said was true.

Eric went on, telling me how impressed he was that I spent what must have been countless hours learning all I did about him. I thought about telling him how I learned what I did, but since I wasn't sure I could even explain it, decided against it. In fact, as I sat there, I realized how big of a risk I took in relying on getting such important information in my dreams. I figured I must have been out of my mind to have even considered doing that. But I was really glad I had done it and wondered if perhaps we all truly were connected at a deep level. *Maybe the only thing that's truly impossible is to understand what's possible,* I thought to myself.

"You still with me, Scott?"

Eric's voice brought me out of my contemplation, and I simply replied that Karine had taught me a lot about connecting with people.

I was curious about something that I couldn't contain and blurted out a question that I'm sure he never expected me to ask. "What ever happened to you and Grace?"

He opened his eyes and mouth as he smiled. "No one knows about her. You're good." Maintaining his smile, he turned away to reminisce. "She and I kept in touch for a few years after I left for California, but then it just fizzled out. It really was a beautiful relationship, but I have no regrets."

I would have enjoyed sharing and learning more, but since I knew he was a very busy man, I felt that we did need to change the subject to discuss his account. Eric explained that he wanted to meet again before he made a decision on whether to give us his business. I thought we really hit it off, but I understood. This was a very big deal, and he was not just representing himself but also a group of partners who trusted him. I quickly figured that my bonus from it would be nearly seven figures, which was bigger than all others I've gotten over the years, combined. It would change my life, dramatically, but to be true to his agenda, I knew I couldn't push him.

He suggested that in a week or so, we go for a ride on the subway and have our next talk while we headed nowhere in particular. I thought that was very creative and fascinating, but not as fascinating as hearing myself say, "That sounds like fun. Let's do it!"

I was hungry and figured he was as well. I also took advantage of something I learned the night before. "How about an early dinner? I know a great Puerto Rican place and don't ask me how I know it, but I believe you like that cuisine."

"I won't ask, yes I do, and I'm starving, but one of us should take off our tie so we don't freak everyone out."

"Actually," I said, "I was thinking we'd leave them on for the exact same reason."

"Man, I knew I'd like you!" he said as we stood up and shared a warm handshake.

The waitress introduced herself to Eric as "Ava," and I was glad she did. I had always called her "the waitress" or "ma'am." I was sure she had mentioned her name before, but I didn't remember it.

It was another long and interesting chat, as we sat, our polka-dotted ties now loose around our necks, sharing our own memories while creating new ones, together. Toward the end of our dinner, I started looking at my watch, believing that I'd demonstrated enough of the personal COO that was required to get me into the first portal. I was optimistic that I would create another great memory after I went to bed that night.

10

There they were, all five of them, and I felt more than ready to jump through to my first portal experience. The border of the first of the five was glowing with a bright and penetrating light. I walked to it and tried to put my hand through. Blocked again. At first I was surprised, but then I recalled something Karine had said about the key to success.

I snapped my fingers, and the polka-dotted tie appeared in my hand. I tied it around my neck and again tested the portal. This time, I saw my hand disappear up to my elbow. I pulled it back for a second, took a deep breath, and stepped through.

I zipped though some sort of tunnel until I saw a bright light ahead. I'd spent only a few seconds in the tunnel but felt that I'd traveled very far. When I reached the end, I stopped moving and looked ahead to see an ancient city in the distance. I assumed it was

Rome, since what looked like the Colosseum was in my line of sight. There was a light misty rain falling, and the sky was decorated with many clouds, including a few darker ones right above me.

I began walking around within a small village, passing through a large area with open-air shops around its perimeter. There were many people walking near me, most wearing sandals and dressed in tunics, yet no one seemed to notice me or care that I was there. I thought they should have, as I was wearing what would have been for them some very unconventional articles of clothing, including the now extremely inappropriate necktie. I took in the scene and then tried to figure out what to do.

This world within the portal seemed even more real than the places I visited in other dreams I'd had. It had such a different quality to it that I checked my watch, almost expecting it to be working. It wasn't.

The mild rain stopped as the darker clouds drifted away from the village. Ahead of me was a circle of benches filled with people, all gathered around a small boy who sat cross-legged on the ground in the center of the circle. I felt a magnetic pull forward.

Without looking at me, he raised his hand and waved me over to him. As I approached him, all the others disappeared. When I was close enough, I sat on the ground next to him. Almost immediately, I had the feeling I first had when I met the beggar. It was him, but he was now the small boy. I put my hands together in prayer position. He let out a small laugh and asked me to just sit with him.

"I wondered if I'd ever see you again," I said.

"How likely is it that more rain will come?" he asked.

"I . . . I don't know," I said. "I feel like it's taken me forever to find you."

"How long do you think it will take for you to find you?" asked the boy.

He seemed to be about eight or nine years old. He had long dark brown hair and wore broken sandals and a small white tunic with a crimson border. I could feel the glow within him as I had back on the street in New York. It was amazing. He didn't confirm his identity, but I needed no confirmation. I felt braver than the first time we met and I jumped right in.

"What is this portal, and why am I here?"

"Portal?" He appeared to ponder the word. "Portal. Yes, I really like that!" he said. "This is the Portal of Awareness."

"Awareness? Awareness of what?" I asked.

"Yes," he replied, "and also of who, where, when, how, and why. It is about seeing what is, not the illusion created from the mind. Here you will get the answers to some of your questions and, more likely, questions about what you believe are some of your answers."

I contemplated the thought as a small salamander stopped in front of us. It was long and thin with greenish smooth skin. Its eyes seemed large in relation to the rest of its body. It looked directly at me, and I got the impression that it was trying to tell me something. I tried to figure out the meaning of it but couldn't. It was as if the clouds that were overhead before were suddenly now *in* my head, blocking me from thinking clearly.

"What is happening to me?"

"You're testing your awareness. How did you do?"

"I think I failed."

He laughed with a sound that I didn't expect to hear coming from a young boy's body. "Oh, that's a good one! I said 'test' and so you decided that you either passed or failed. How fascinating."

With that, he reached out his small hand, and the salamander jumped onto his palm. He brought it to his cheek and rubbed it against him. He then returned it to the ground, and it ran away. I was completely baffled by the whole encounter and felt as if I was missing the point.

"What does this all mean?" I asked.

"What do you mean by 'this'?"

"This village, here, now. The salamander. Wait, I am dreaming, right?"

"You are asking a question to which you would not yet understand the answer. However, I will indulge you. Yes, you are dreaming. You have been dreaming all your life. You just do not remember."

He was right. I was more confused than before I'd asked the question. "Do you mean that up until recently, I have not been able to remember my dreams?"

"I mean," he said, "that every aspect of your life is a dream, and that you do not remember who you are and why you are here."

He stopped and looked up. "I am just not sure if it will rain again, what do you think? I like the rain." Now he sounded like a young boy.

"I really don't know if it will rain," I felt I needed to say and did so. I then added, "I'm not sure what you mean about every aspect of my life being a dream."

When he responded, he no longer sounded like a small boy. "It is a challenging concept. Just think about it, or perhaps consider *not* thinking about it." We both laughed, but as was once the case with Lucena, I was unsure of what was funny.

He stood and dusted himself off. "When you dream, you are unaware that it is not reality. How real do your dreams feel to you?"

I stood then, too, and wiped the dirt from my pants. "They feel very real. So nothing in the world is real?"

"Let us just say that the world is an illusion, but your experience of it is real. So, it is not real, and it is not unreal."

I chewed on that for a while but wasn't ready to swallow.

"Allow me to ask you a question," he said. "How do you know that you are not just a dream character within someone else's dream?"

Suddenly the dark clouds moved over us again and it started to rain. This time, it was coming down much harder than before.

When it did, the boy began dancing around in a circle with his arms in the air, his head tilted back, and his tongue stretched out to taste the raindrops.

"Hey!" he said excitedly, as if he'd just discovered a cure for blindness. "Want to jump the drops?"

"What do you mean?"

"Come on!" he said, waving for me to join him.

Just then the rain stopped. And when I say stopped, I mean that literally. The raindrops just stopped all at once in midair, suspended where they were. He jumped up on a single drop with one foot and another drop with the other. He then began jumping around on different drops, one by one, up and down, yelling the whole time as if he was on an amusement park ride. He then stopped on a pair of drops, balancing his weight by holding out his arms like a tightrope walker.

He turned his head to me. "What are you waiting for? Come on!"

"I can't do that."

"Why not?" he asked, curiously.

"I just can't."

"Okay. No worries." As if he was riding a bucking bronco, he held one hand onto an invisible rope and raised the other over his head as he rode the two drops until he dropped down to the ground in front of me. As he did, the clouds departed, taking the rain with them.

"Come with me," he said, offering his hand to me as he'd done to the salamander. When I grabbed it, he snapped two fingers of his other hand, and we were then hovering about thirty feet over the center of the Colosseum. Below us, hundreds of spectators raptly watched two warriors engaged in a heated battle.

One of the gladiators threw a trident at the other, impaling the man through his abdomen and pinning him to a wall. He screamed out in pain and tried to break free of the wall as the first gladiator walked slowly toward him, drawing his sword.

"What do you see?" asked the boy.

I could barely answer as I stared in horror. "He's going to kill him! Can we stop him?" I asked in a panic.

The boy held my hand, and we flew out of the Colosseum and then over the village, setting down in a deeply wooded and serene area. There were two smooth and comfortable rocks, and we each sat on one and watched a single leaf float from right to left on a small babbling brook. Amazingly, my torment about the gladiators seemed to float away on the leaf as it passed us, leaving me immersed in the beauty of the moment.

"What do you see?" he again asked me.

I felt a tear beginning to form. "This is so beautiful. The movement of the water. The leaf. The sound of the brook. Just beautiful."

"Ah, but this is no different from what you observed in the Colosseum," he stated.

"Of course it's different. That was violent and horrible, and this is beautiful."

"Nothing is as it appears to you to be," he said. "Everything just is."

"Is what? You must be seeing something very different from what I see," I mused.

"The only difference between us is that I know who I am, and you do not yet remember who you are."

"Who are you?" I asked.

"I am Awareness. I see everything."

"Are you saying that I am Awareness as well?"

"Only when you remember. I'll be here when you are ready to see again."

"Wait, what do you mean?"

6:59.

11

Karine had set up my next meeting with Eric Concord. She also chose where we were to meet: the newly opened 96th Street Second Avenue Subway stop. The morning of the meeting, I decided to have another heart-to-heart conversation with her.

"You've done very well, Scott. Concord is extremely impressed with you."

"Thanks. Wouldn't have done it without you. I appreciated the very gentle nudge, by the way." She laughed. "And yes, I remember our deal. As soon as I see Nowell next, I'll set something up with him."

"Oh, no need to make that effort," she said, confusing me a bit. "I've already set up dinner for the two of you at Las Puertas." You'll find it on your schedule. I know that Nowell likes that place as well."

"That's either extremely efficient or extremely pushy," I laughed. "Either way, thanks. Can I ask you a question?" I waved her over to the window. "Please look out here with me and tell me what you see."

Karine looked up and down and absorbed the scene before responding. "I see a world. A world of opportunity."

"If you don't mind, I'm curious; what do you think about when I say the word awareness?"

"Scott, what's gotten into you?"

"What do you mean?"

"Something's different about you. I'm not exactly sure what it is, but it's there for sure, and . . ." she paused for a moment, looking closely at me, "I like it."

"Well, I don't feel very different, but I don't feel the same, either."

"That's what I mean. You seem more . . . open, if that's the right word." She paused again. "Anyway, being aware, to me, is the ability to see the world and all the people in it as it is and they are, not as we want it or them to be."

This answer had a different feel to it than her other answer. This one not only made sense conceptually, but something within my body seemed to resonate with it.

"Now that's really cool. When you said that you saw a world of opportunity, did you mean that's your reality?"

"Yeah, I think so. I mean, we can believe anything we want, right? So, I choose to believe that, yes."

When I looked up to contemplate what she said, I saw Damon making a beeline to my office. Karine must have seen my eyes widen in anticipation, for she stood right up and walked out the door, past him.

He stood at my doorway and began speaking. "Scott, I heard you met with Concord. When I found out about it, I figured you were out of your mind." He paused to see my reaction, then went on after none was forthcoming. "But I heard from one of Concord's partners that you did a fair job. All I want to say is—and believe me, I'm serious about this—*do not* screw it up. I hope you understand."

"Damon, what do you see?" I asked with a flair of confidence and curiosity that seemed to startle him for a second. He didn't take too long to answer, though.

"Honestly? I see a guy who has a ton of talent, wasting all of it because he just doesn't care anymore."

"Thanks for your honest answer, and yes, I do think I know what you're saying."

He took a long, hard look at me, then turned and walked away without saying another word.

* * *

I took a cab to 96th and Second Avenue, swiped my MetroCard, and made my way down the stairs to the platform. Like many New Yorkers, I was fascinated by the history of the Second Avenue Subway. First planned in the 1920s, the project was still not finished almost a hundred years later. The 96th Street station, recently opened, was refreshingly clean and decorated with nice artwork.

Eric had apparently beaten me there, and he yelled "Hey, buddy!" as I approached the outer edge of the bustling crowd.

I waved and wove my way through the masses to reach him. "Ready?" he asked.

"I'm more than ready," I replied. The Q train was already at the station, so we boarded and miraculously found two empty seats next to each other as the train left the station, heading toward Coney Island.

"What's new in your world, Scott?"

I thought about asking which world he was referring to, but instead simply replied, "Nothing much, Eric. Just trying to figure out the meaning of life."

He laughed. "I know the drill. Ask questions, get no answers, ask again, and still get no answers. Then for the fun of it, ask again and expect answers."

This time I laughed. "Thought I was the only one!"

He sat back in the molded plastic seat and took a more serious tone. "I know my account means a lot to your company and a lot of money to you, and as you would expect, I've been giving it all a lot of thought. I'm not quite ready to make a decision though, because there is a potential challenge with your team."

"Oh, really?" I said, not expecting him to say what I was actually thinking, which he did.

"It's Damon. I really don't know about that guy. The word on the street is that he's a bit of a shyster. I don't get the sense that you and Karine are like that, but Damon's reputation precedes him. What's your take on that?"

"I guess I'm supposed to make something up and convince you to think otherwise, but I just don't know how to do that, and you deserve much more." I paused when the next stop was announced. I didn't understand a word that was said over the train's sound system, but everyone else seemed clear, with a few rising to the occasion.

"I've known Damon since college, and he got me this job. To be honest, we don't see eye to eye about much these days, but deep down he really is a good person. But I will tell you this; if you trust me with this account, I promise that I will take care of your business as if it were my own. If anything even remotely begins to look off to me, you will know about it within sixty seconds. Karine's the same way; you can trust her with your life. I've never spoken with a single client who didn't love her."

"So that brings me to my point. I'm not sure how to ask this except directly. Have you ever considered starting your own firm? With Karine?"

Did he just suggest that if I left the firm that I could have his entire account? "Wow, Eric, I . . ."

I stopped in midsentence, feeling a pang of terror as I spotted the stranger outside on the platform. He was standing still, facing me, black cap on, head down. I wasn't sure how he could possibly see me, but as the train began pulling away, he turned, head still down, to follow my path.

"What the hell are you looking at?" I heard from behind me.

I turned quickly, startled more by what I just heard than by the man in the black cap. Eric's wording exactly echoed what I'd said to Karine in my dream when she was spying on me. "I'm sorry, Eric. What did you just say?"

"I asked if you were okay. You seem distracted."

"I . . . I thought you said something else." I turned back to the platform, but it was no longer in sight. "I'm . . . okay."

"You sure, man?"

"I am. Thanks."

I sat quietly for the next several minutes. Eric followed my lead and relaxed. We both knew that I'd get back to his question when I was ready to discuss it with him.

"Hey, Eric?"

"Yeah?"

"What do you see?"

"Intriguing question." He put his hand on his chin and paused before continuing. He gestured at the young woman seated across from us. "I see a mother of three who is looking forward to getting home to her family. She was at a doctor's appointment and isn't yet sure of her prognosis and won't be until the results from the test she just took come in. But she is sure of who she loves and will greet them with a giant hug."

My mouth opened and formed a half-smile. If I didn't know better, I'd have thought that he actually knew the woman.

"Her kids won't have a clue as to why she's squeezing them so hard, and they will complain that she's hurting them. She won't care and will hold them for as long as she can," he said.

He pointed to a couple. "See them? They're going to be married in a few months. They just picked out their wedding cake and are living in their own world. I could go sit right in front of them and snap my fingers in their faces, and they wouldn't even know I was there."

I was caught a little off guard with his use of the phrase "snap my fingers."

"Oh, and that's Sam." He tilted his head toward a middle-aged man sitting three seats down on his left, wearing a scarf and a heavy coat that didn't fit him very well. "Sam is wondering whether his wife is cheating on him and left work early to see if he can confirm his suspicions."

"I see," I said, with a tone of appreciation. "That's it? Just a few people on a train, huh?"

"Of course not. Look straight in front of us."

I did and saw nothing except the window, the silver subway doors, and a large advertisement for a Broadway show overhead. "I don't see anyone," I said.

"You don't?" he said, surprised. "Well, I do. I see factory workers operating machines that cut sheets of stainless steel into intricate shapes before they're made into the pieces of this subway car. I see their families waiting for them to come home at the end of the day. I see the foreman whose job it is to make sure everything is just right. He knows that people like us will be riding in his train and will rely on him for their safety. Actually, looking even more closely, I see people mining raw materials to make that stainless steel, and still others completing the process of forming the sheets before they're shipped to the factory."

Eric was just warming up.

"See that window? It's made of shatterproof glass. I see the many glass workers, cutting the glass to size, and others carefully inspecting it to make sure that it's perfect. I see those workers in school, being inspired by their teachers, who helped shape their futures. And I see their teachers, working countless hours to prepare lesson plans."

"Wow, Eric," I said, "that's incredible."

"No, it's really simple. I just look past my story and, instead, into what I can imagine is theirs. You have to look at the big picture." He paused and then produced a hearty laugh. "No, I mean *literally*. You try it. Just look at that big picture over there and tell me what you see."

I sat back and put my hand on my chin like a detective, ogling the Broadway play ad. Instead of just making something up, I tried to imagine that the picture was telling me a story and that what I was saying was true. "Hmm," I said with a child-like tone in my voice. "Okay. I got this. I see hundreds of actors and actresses, some experienced and some with a dream to land their first role, all auditioning with the hopes of being selected for the play. I see them as children, around the age of six, pretending to be different characters as they performed for their parents. They persevered, while others became discouraged and gave up. I see people building the sets of the play, ushering in guests, and selling tickets. I see the playwright spending hours toiling over every word in the script."

"Well, then. I see you being pretty amazing, yourself."

We played this game for the next hour or so, fascinating and amusing each other. We must have looked a little strange to the other passengers. One even went so far as to move a few seats further away from us, which made us burst into laughter.

We decided to jump out at the next-to-last stop and take a train back to where we started. We were relatively quiet on the way back, just enjoying the sights.

"Eric, thank you. This was an enlightening experience. I'll never look at a train the same way again. Actually, I'm not sure if I'll look at anything in quite the same way again."

"You're welcome, Scott. And I really want you to think about what I asked you. I have to take a trip out West for a little while and would like to meet for dinner when I return. I will be ready to make a decision then."

"I will think very seriously about what you're proposing, and I'll be ready when you're back. You pick the place this time. Just let me know where and when. Oh, and by the way, I want you to do whatever is best for you, and if that's me being your business associate, great. If not, then I'd at least want to remain friends." Eric looked closely into my eyes, nodded slowly, and went on his way.

The meeting had taken much longer than I expected, and I was surprised to see Karine waiting for me when I returned to the office. "Well, how did it go?" she asked.

"I think it went well, but he did bring up something very interesting and unexpected." I told Karine about the conversation regarding Damon as well as Eric's suggestion that we start our own firm. Her eyes lit up with anticipation.

"Scott! That's amazing. You're going to say we will, right? Scott?"

"I don't know what I'm going to say, Karine. I really don't know."

12

It was nearly one in the morning, and I couldn't sleep. I had really enjoyed the game that Eric and I played but was still a little shaken by my thoughts of the near encounter with the man in the black cap. I took an old sleeping pill that I found in my night table, hoping it would help me drift off to the dream world.

It was the middle of the night in the village by the Colosseum. Only a few lanterns lit the way toward the open area where I expected to find the boy. I wasn't disappointed. He was seated within the same circle as before. He was by himself, waiting for me.

"Welcome back," he said.

"Wasn't sure I'd make it here tonight." I looked around and noticed that there were fewer lanterns in one particular area. The boy took notice of my curiosity.

"What do you see?" he asked.

This time, I was prepared. "I see lanterns, each made by the hand of a villager who learned the skill from his father, and he from his father's father. They are all humbly sharing themselves in the only way they know how. I see the people who carefully hung them there and how they, as well, learned to do that from their elders when they were just teens. I see . . ."

The boy snapped his fingers and the lanterns went out.

"What do you see?" he asked again.

"I . . . can't see. It's completely dark."

"What if you tried seeing without using your eyes?"

I was confused, but after a short few moments, I relaxed and began to talk. "Yes. I see. I see the darkness that uses the wind to whisper its story to me. It understands its purpose, for it knows that the cloak it wears will soon drop into the morning sun's rays." As I spoke, I felt the now-familiar feeling that, although I was speaking, the words coming from my mouth were not mine—or, perhaps more literally, not of my mind.

"What have you learned so far?"

"That my perceptions have been limiting me and that there's more to see than meets the eye. Even in the dark."

"We each see what we expect to see," said the boy. "Our outer view is a reflection and projection of our inner view. If you expect darkness, you will be in the dark."

"How can I see things as they truly are?"

"Ah," said the boy, "that takes some time. All your life, you've been seeing your own version of reality. At least right now you are seeing past your prior assumptions. Continue the practice of looking deep into the story of what you see. Just keep asking, what am I really seeing? Do not just accept what your past or your senses tell you. Question *everything*, curiously, including whatever *I* tell you."

He paused and then continued, "I like what you said about the dark, as 'seeing' is a whole experience. By the way," he added, "I also liked the exercise you did on the train. That showed me that you are being much more present; you were seeing beyond the image in front of you and into the depth of the picture."

"How do you know about the game we played?"

"There is only one world, Scott; just different dimensions of it. Hey, what's all this discussion around darkness!" He snapped his fingers, illuminating the sun from within the night's sky. He then offered me his hand.

We walked beside a river, observing workers already engaged in backbreaking morning activities of collecting mud from the river-bank. Others sweated profusely as they mixed the mud with straw and water to form the mud-bricks that were used to build houses. The boy picked up a shovel and began collecting mud and putting it in a container. One of the workers handed me a digging spade and, polka-dotted tie and all, I worked to dig a trench. As I did, the boy began singing a song I'd never heard before. Listening to him sing, I wondered how it was possible for me to create things in my dream that I'd never heard of in my waking life.

"You did well before on the train and with the darkness. They were beautiful first steps. This time, however, try something differ-ent. As you see yourself and others in this field, continue to let go of your past assumptions and now try to let go of any current interpretations and creative stories. Instead, just see. No thoughts at all."

"Yes, I see what you mean," I said, acknowledging him without immediately realizing the obvious play on words.

"What questions do you have?" asked the boy, as I watched him breathe a little heavier from the hard labor.

For the life of me, I couldn't think of a single one. My mind was occupied only by the feel of the mud between the toes of my now bare feet and some water that slowly seeped into the trench I was digging. The midmorning sun began to burn our bodies.

When I felt the sweat dripping from my forehead and touched my drenched shirt with my hand, my mind re-engaged and I started wondering how people ever did this kind of work for more than a few minutes. But as I looked around, people seemed much more content than I was, and I began feeling very foolish about how I'd been complaining about my life.

"Tired?" asked the boy. I was, both physically and mentally, and had a little trouble answering. He dropped his shovel and, instead of transporting us somewhere, pointed down at the trench I had just dug up. It was completely filled with water, rippling from a slight breeze.

As I stared at the trench, thoughts of the heat, the workers, my own exhaustion, and other random things, including my self-judgments, began to fade.

He got on his hands and knees and looked into the trench and said, "See."

I knelt next to him. I no longer felt as if I was in a dream, but I wasn't quite awake either. I looked at the image of my watch reflected in the water. I could see that the second hand was stopped, yet the slow movement of the water distorted the watch face to make the watch look like it was moving. So it was not working, but also working. At that moment, I was so confused about what was real, the fact that my watch could at once be working and not working actually made sense.

I continued to stare at the water as the wind stopped and the surface of the water went still. A new image began to appear. It was several years earlier, and I was in my office, having a wonderfully engaged discussion with a potential client.

"Wow," I said to the boy, "I really did have some passion in me back then." I watched as the client shook my hand and thanked me.

Just then, the wind again picked up, and ripples formed in the water, erasing one image so that a new one could come into focus as the water again went still as glass. The image was one of an event that had happened several weeks later, with the same client storming out of my office in disgust. Damon had made a bad investment decision that led to a significant loss of money for the client. As per Damon's request, which I'd heard as a demand, I'd claimed full responsibility for what happened, but that mattered little to the soon-to-be ex-client. After he stormed out, I watched myself sink into my chair and put my head in my hands.

The scene faded, and I continued to stare at the water as I spoke. "And that's when I lost the fire," I added after a long pause. "So, is part of being aware learning from the pain of the past?" I asked.

"Being aware is simply about seeing. What you do with what you see is up to you. The more aware you are, the less fooled you will be by the illusions of the mind, with its built-in expectations that shape what you are looking at. The less fooled you are, the more open you are to seeing the absolute perfection of reality; of seeing the whole of Consciousness. I asked you to look into the trench to face a memory that has tainted the view of your current reality."

"So, my past is influencing my current view of reality. I understand. So, what else do I need to know about awareness?" I asked, hoping to be able to graduate to the next portal.

"What else?" he chuckled. "You do not know anything yet! There is a very big difference between being aware and being Awareness. We have only discussed being aware, which is just seeing what is."

The boy continued, "Being aware is also, as you pointed out in the dark, seeing what is not apparently visible. It is seeing with all of your senses, outer and inner. Whether it's the texture of sand on the shore of your favorite beach, the sound of a newborn's cry, the message in your life's lessons, or the nature of reality, there are more things to be aware of than there are stars in the entire universe.

"Awareness is different. On the most basic level, the fact that a part of you is aware of anything means that even though no one can point to it or find it within your brain, Awareness exists as reality. If that's all you are able to comprehend for now, that is fine."

"And if I want to understand it even more deeply . . . ?"

"To understand Awareness at its deepest level, you would need to go beyond that logic and listen to the part of you that knows the unlimited nature of Awareness. You will come to know Awareness as a permanent state unto itself. Awareness isn't an aspect, attribute, or action of anything else. It is a state of being—*the* state of Being. If being aware is seeing, then Awareness is sight.

"Awareness is the nature of reality. It is the true Observer, observing you, the observed. Awareness is always aware. Always and in all ways."

"So before, I was being more aware. How can I be Awareness?" I asked.

"Being aware is about *what* and *how* you see. Being Awareness is about understanding *who* is seeing. To be Awareness, you have to awaken to your True Nature, that you are the seer.

"Also, Awareness is not some *thing*; it is everything. Awareness is synonymous with your True Essence; it is the eye of Consciousness; the vision of God. Since Consciousness is all there is and so it is also all that can be seen, the answer to the question 'What do you see?' is, ultimately, 'I Am.'"

"I've heard of the term 'I Am' before, many times, but I'd like to hear your explanation of it."

"I Am is Consciousness. Pure Existence. All encompassing; nothing else. Think of it this way: When you looked in a mirror when you were a child, you saw a different self than you saw when you were a teenager. You see another when you look in the mirror now. You have always paid attention to the 'self' you saw, but not to the "I' that saw that self. Regardless of the many different selves you saw, the 'I' that saw them was always there, always in the background, always observing, always exactly the same. It was always the only self that was permanent. It was the 'I Am.'"

"I never thought of it like that. Very interesting. You also said Awareness was the eye of Consciousness. What do you mean?"

"Human beings do not *have* a body and mind; humans *are* a body and mind. Without a body and mind, there is no human being. It will help you to understand reality better by thinking that various aspects or elements, when combined, make Consciousness what it is. The teachings of the portals will help you experience those various aspects. This journey will help you *mentally* comprehend Consciousness; however, because your mind thinks in relative, or relational, terms, it has an intrinsic limitation in that it can understand the parts, but not the whole. So even though I describe the words Awareness and Consciousness separately, because everything that is, is Consciousness, Consciousness does not *have* Awareness; it *is* Awareness. Consciousness is not something to become; it is something to be reclaimed."

"I'm beginning to see what you are saying," I said, "and for me to better understand it now, I also guess that there's a difference between being conscious and Consciousness."

The boy nodded. "People often confuse the two concepts. You can use the term being conscious to describe your level of lucidity. You can *become* more conscious, just as you can *become* more aware. You can even think of your level of consciousness as how conscious you are of Consciousness.

"I know all of this can be confusing, and my objective is not for you to completely understand what I am saying yet. It is only to say what I have to say and know that sooner or later, whenever you are ready, it will resonate within you."

"It *is* confusing, but there's something soothing about it to me. I just wish I better understood the words you're using," I said.

"Perhaps you will understand Consciousness through other terms that you've learned: the Universe, Being, Higher Self, God, and many other words. All of those words mean the same thing, and yet Consciousness is a thing, and no thing, as it is unlimited. It is your True Essence as absolute, infinite, and ineffable. Consciousness experiences itself through Awareness, the Observer."

"And what does it observe?" I asked.

"Perhaps you would like to see for yourself?" he replied. I nodded, and he went on. "Imagine stepping outside of yourself and observing. Just watch a movie starring a man called Scott. Do not make any interpretations, just observe, curiously. That will give you more of an idea of what is known as the Observer."

"I understand the concept, but it is still hard to grasp as truth."

"Let me ask you a question, Scott. Who watches your dreams?"

"My mind?"

"Your mind creates the images, but it is not the watcher. Think of it this way. You purposely fall asleep, and you dream. Consciousness also chooses to experience the 'fall,' in that it purposely falls asleep to its infinite nature and enters the finite dream world. That is your world, Scott; that is where you live. The I Am creates that world to experience the experience of life . . . through you.

"You are now experiencing a lucid dream. A dream created by Scott's mind. The outer world you think you know is also a lucid dream, dreamt up by the One Dreamer, Consciousness itself."

"I don't understand why Consciousness would want to create a dream."

"Until you are dreaming, any particular dream exists only as one of unlimited possibilities. When you enter into a dream, the endless possibilities collapse into one particular limited experience. All experiences are temporary dreams. Consciousness, by falling asleep, collapses its unlimited Self into a limited focus: a limited dream self, in this case, the self known as Scott."

"But why would it need to do that? Why would Consciousness need to do anything at all?"

"Something can only be recognized by its opposite. In order for light to know itself, it must experience darkness. This gives light a context for reflection. To know all that it is, Consciousness chooses to experience all that it is not. Since it cannot do that in the absolute, it creates a dream, a world with comparisons. A world of duality. It knows *its* light by living *your* darkness, Scott. This is a perfect process of remembering. In that process, the self reveals the *Self*.

"Look all around you. What can you actually see?"

"I can see everything that is all around me," I replied.

"Actually, that is not the case. You have a sense of the things around you, but unless you focus on any particular thing, everything is blurry. Consciousness is aware of itself as unlimited, as everything, but only because it limits its view by creating a narrow focus within its dream world. By temporarily limiting its view, it knows itself in comparison to its unlimited nature. Without your human eyes, Consciousness would be blurry."

"Consciousness creates a dream world and I create one, too? And I also have a waking world? How many worlds are there?" I asked.

"Not two," was his response.

"Not two?"

"What you see and know is limited by what your mind can see and know. For now, understand this: You are not who you think you are. You are awakening to Truth—removing the blinders from your eyes. You will eventually know that you are the observer and the participant; the dream and the Dreamer."

"Wait," I jumped in. "I remember something from when we were on the sidewalk. At one point, I felt I was everything and nothing at the same time."

"Yes, you were remembering some of your True Essence."

"I want to feel that again. Can you help me?"

"Learn the lessons of the portals. They are a path to enlightenment, to seeing the light of Truth. That is what you truly want and are being pulled toward."

"Yes, I've been feeling that pull since I first saw the light. It's like a powerful craving. What is that?"

"The truth lies within your core, pulling you away from the illusion. You felt the pull toward the light from your office window, toward Lucena, toward the first portal you saw, and toward me. These were all caused by your Essence beginning to awaken to the truth, remembering yourself as pure Consciousness."

"So lucid dreaming is the way to Truth?"

"It doesn't matter that you chose to become lucid in your dreams. You could have meditated or adopted any other method or discipline for awakening. Some people look to religion for an answer. Some study metaphysics. Some explore philosophy or science. Some listen to the voice within, and some prefer to listen to other's voices. The path does not matter. The reality is that even the concept of awakening is just another illusion. Your True Essence is always awake, even if you are unaware of it.

"Now make an intention toward your Self. Because you understand what it means to be awake in *your* dreams, you can begin to discover what it's like to be awake in *the* dream. You do see the irony, though, right? You went to sleep to awaken."

"This is a lot to consider," I said.

"What is one thing that you can now see?"

"I am more than I can possibly imagine."

We held hands again and were back over the Colosseum.

"What do you see?"

"That I am aware."

"What is the nature of that which is aware?"

"I Am."

He took the sandals off his feet, and they grew to my size. "These will be the key to the next portal—a reminder that life is a journey and to tread lightly on your perceptions."

When I woke up, I felt another strong pull; a desire to remember my Essence. I took out my journal and went to a blank page and titled the page with the first idea that popped up:

Uncovering the Truth

Portal 1—Aware is what we can be. Awareness is the way of Being.

13

As I went about my business over the next few days, I practiced observing my life as if it were a movie. From that detached perspective, I was better able to see how much drama I, and the people around me, created every day. I was amazed at the stories I made up without realizing I did so. I guess I did pretty well with the awareness lesson, because when Portal 2 appeared before me, I passed right through it.

It took me a while to figure out where I was, which was in a huge tent. There were loud noises outside and people moving quickly inside. When I heard the unforgettable blast of a nearby bomb, I knew there was a war going on. There was a nurse in front of me, holding out a pair of combat boots.

"Come on! Put these on. People are dying. Let's move!" she yelled.

When she handed me the boots, I looked in her eyes and saw the beggar. He was now a nurse with braided brown hair tied up in a bun. She wore light blue scrubs that were spotted with blood. There were many beds within the tent and several nurses and doctors, also in blood-splattered scrubs. As I put the boots on, my entire outfit was transformed and I, too, was in similar apparel.

"Grab that tray," she ordered.

"What are we doing here?" I asked.

"The tray, and follow me."

The nurse moved from one side of the tent to the other, passing many soldiers writhing in pain, as well as a few still ones with sheets over their heads. We stopped at a bed that held a soldier with one leg bloodied and shredded below the knee. He screamed out in agony. Another medic ran over to help, hooking the soldier up to an IV. Within a few moments, he was still visibly in pain, but much calmer.

"Hand me that bandage. The big one."

I looked on the tray and grabbed what I thought she wanted. She used it like a tourniquet and wrapped it around what remained of his bloodied leg. She then asked me to help her hold the man down while someone else took a saw and raised it above the soldier's kneecap. I realized he was about to begin cutting and I felt my own knees weakening.

The next thing I remember was sitting outside the tent on a blanket, watching many planes flying in random patterns across the distant sky. I imagined all the people who were injured or killed in the war, and I began to feel a deep sense of grief.

The nurse came out of the tent, removed her plastic gloves, walked toward me, and sat down. She looked at the sky, closed her eyes, and took a deep breath.

"What do you make of all this?"

"Tragic. Just hard to believe what we do to each other," I said.

"Do you believe it is bad?"

"Well of course I do. Who wouldn't?"

"Maybe the question should be *what* wouldn't? Take my hand, please."

We disappeared and instantly reappeared on the boardwalk at the beach where I had my first lucid dream.

Right in front of me, a seagull dropped a large crab on one of the boardwalk's slats. They faced each other in what appeared to be an impending battle. Then they froze like the raindrops in the first portal. Everything other than the nurse and me was frozen in time. Even other birds were suspended in midair. My thoughts at this point had changed from wondering if I was creating *all* of my dream content to wondering whether I created *any* of it.

"What are they thinking?"

"I have no idea," I said.

"Everyone and everything is connected. What if you thought with their minds instead of with yours?"

I began imagining that I was the bird. I remembered the lesson about seeing and didn't want to create a story. "What do I see?" I asked myself.

I closed my eyes and took a breath. I felt a connection and then just blurted out a hunch. "The bird is deciding where to strike. It wants to make sure it doesn't get within the range of the claws." I stopped to try to feel more deeply. "Nothing else." I opened my eyes and turned to the nurse "I have no other thoughts."

"Now experience the crab. Go even deeper this time."

I closed my eyes again. It took a few moments to tune myself in to what felt like the crab's experience.

"The crab, it's . . . I'm . . . I'm not thinking, exactly . . . I'm feeling . . . stimulation . . . excitement. But not in a good or bad way. I'm just ready for battle." I opened my eyes again. "The crab is operating on instinct."

Just then, everything became reanimated. The battle was over very quickly. The gull was way too powerful for the crab. It wasn't even a fight.

"So, what is the difference between that battle and the one from our last stop?"

"Well, I think the gull and crab were just doing what they do, living, eating, dying. Surviving or not. Nothing more. But people feel fear, anger, worry, hatred, and a lot of other things."

"So you are saying that the animals did not display judgment?" she asked.

"Yes, I guess that's what I'm saying. Only humans do. It was a natural event for the animals." I paused before continuing. "Maybe it's not correct to say that it's unnatural for humans, but it feels that way."

"Nature is natural, and we are all nature. We all do what we are instinctually programmed to do. Everyone fights—animals to nourish or protect themselves, and humans for the same purpose. There is no difference except your viewpoint of the two experiences."

"But humans have a choice. They don't have to kill, which they often do out of anger, stemming from judgment," I said.

"We all want pleasure and we all seek to remove pain, and we will kill for either. Until we raise our level of consciousness by understanding the idea that we are all One, we will continue to perpetuate our ancestor's conditioning, which tells us to kill or be killed. You are correct that most people judge and so live from old ideas instead of new ones. In that sense, most people are just sleepwalking in a nightmare from which they are not yet ready to awaken.

"Keep something in mind, though; all beings are on a journey. All journeys are part of a normal, natural process. They all lead to Consciousness. We are all the same, just at different stages of awakening."

"But I would never kill anyone," I said

"How sure are you of that? Think about what you would do if a loved one was being threatened. We all have our justifications. We all do whatever we can to protect ourselves and our beliefs and what we hold dear to us. If you cannot yet remember that we are all One, remember at least that we are all similar."

I thought about Damon and how I judged him and how hard it would be not to. I wondered how I could ever just accept him for who he was. The nurse must have read my mind.

"First, know that conflict is derived from fear and that all people are afraid. How can we not be if we do not remember our True Essence?"

She held out her hand, and I was soon in a room full of babies. They all looked pretty much the same.

"Where is the conflict?"

"I see none," I replied.

With a snap of her fingers, I was then with a group of toddlers.

"Tell me about the conflict within these children."

"I still don't see any."

"And you cannot, as they are still relatively pure within their Essence. However, notice that some act differently than others. They are beginning to learn to have their own separate identities: their own way of interacting. They learn that from everyone they encounter as well as from their senses. From there they will develop what comes next, which is an ego."

"Yes, I can understand that," I said.

"The ego creates a sense of self, which continues to separate them even more. Separation causes fear. These toddlers are all learning to be afraid, because they are starting to forget the truth and so, beginning to feel isolated, alone, and vulnerable. They will soon learn to fight to protect themselves. I am not sure if you can understand this yet, but this is a purposeful process. Everything is purposeful, or it would not exist. The children are supposed to forget. Their current experience of isolation and vulnerability will help them awaken to their True Essence as One and invulnerable. We all fall asleep and forget, and we all awaken and remember. That, too, is part of nature, a natural process."

Her fingers snapped again and we found ourselves in a group of slightly older children, perhaps six or seven years old.

"Look at them. Each looks very different now, yet they are all still trying to find their way back to their true nature again. They have forgotten, and so they are lost. Confused. Their world tells them that they are separate and isolated, which is something that they inherently know is untrue. They are caught in the illusion of *self,* and they are learning to be afraid accordingly. That fear is born along with their feeling of separation."

"I can certainly relate to that." I said.

"Everyone can probably relate to that to some degree. From now on, no matter who a person might be, no matter what they might do, know that they are just like all of us, all just young children trying to feel acceptance, peace, and love—all trying to feel safe. Regardless of how it appears, we all want the exact same things, and we are all on the same path. See this, and you will no longer judge others, and no longer judge yourself. See this, and your level of consciousness will move closer to its natural state."

I paused for a moment to consider what she'd said and the idea that we live in a world of our mind's creation. "If it causes us so much trouble, why do we create judgment in our lives?" I then asked.

"The judgments we make are natural consequences from our experiences in a world based on duality and opposites. A world filled with either/or thinking. In fact, think about the babies we saw. They did not yet make any distinctions between themselves and the world around them. Based on their perceptions, their minds inevitably learned to separate themselves from others and judge everything and everyone in comparison to themselves. We are not born into duality; our minds create it."

"So nonjudgment should be my quest?"

"This is the Portal of Acceptance. Unconditional Acceptance. Nonjudgment is required to move toward that, but I would not think of it or anything as a quest or goal. You cannot consider something that is inevitable to be a goal. Awakening to reality is a natural process. It will happen. We all eventually remember. Our only choice is when. For many, it will become more prominent later in their lives. When that occurs, their inner truth will pull them toward wholeness until they awaken to feel it."

"So we all awaken in our lifetimes?"

"That depends on how you define life. I said our choice is about when we awaken. Those who do not make that choice in this 'lifetime' do not awaken within it. Another portal will help you understand your belief about the concept of life."

"Is it even possible to truly experience nonjudgment?"

"When you no longer ask that question, it will be."

"Are you saying that because my mind is limited and I'm asking from within its constraints, I can't understand the concept?"

"You talk about your mind as if it is a possession and describe it as if it is not one with you. The mind only seems to be separate, but it is not. It is one with nature at all times. There is no way that it cannot be, as nothing is truly separate. However, as you have learned before, the mind is the part of you that does not remember the truth, so yes, it will try to stop you because it believes that if you find your True Self, it will lose itself, its identity as Scott."

"So to experience nonjudgment, I must let go of my mind's hold on what it believes is reality."

"Yes, and that may not be easy, but you can take steps toward it by becoming more accepting, one experience at a time."

"Please tell me more about acceptance," I requested.

"If you accept the world fully, there will be no judgment, so there will be no disgust, nor will there be any good or bad outcomes. Think of it this way: When you say accept, you use it in a way that depicts resignation. True Acceptance does not render you a victim. The opposite occurs. Unconditional Acceptance empowers you to see the God in all others. It removes your suffering and brings peace your way."

"And how does acceptance differ from what I learned in the awareness portal?"

"To satisfy your mind, I will tell you that Portal 1 was about seeing without interpretation, meaning seeing without the filters that cloud your sight. This portal is about experiencing what you see without judgment."

"You said before that I can take steps toward becoming more accepting. It would help my mind again if you distinguished between accepting and acceptance."

"As with all states of experience, there is a difference between being accepting of things, which is the mind wanting to *do* something, and being Unconditional Acceptance, which is not about doing; it is a quality of Being, and as you said before, unlike anything you can conceive of with your mind. Like Awareness, true Acceptance is a permanent state. I will help you experience Acceptance when you are better prepared, and for now, remember that being more accepting is a step toward Acceptance."

"I think it would be difficult for me to be even just more accepting. Is it really worth the effort?"

"I will let you answer that question yourself. Consider this: How well do you accept your life, including all that you are, based on all you have experienced, including your upbringing?"

A chill came over me. I'd learned to distinguish between the good chill, the tingling one that begins to warm my body, and the other chill, the one that cools it. This time, I was freezing.

"Imagine what it would be like to relieve yourself of pain that no longer serves you. That would be one benefit, and there are many more. Understand that most of your emotional suffering comes from nonacceptance. Once you unconditionally accept the people, places, and things in your life, you will release yourself from the confinement created from deep within your mind that keeps you stuck in the illusion of a painful, unjust, and disappointing world.

"Surrender, Scott. First see and then surrender to what is. Let go. Let it be."

I thought about my job, the relationship issues, my fears and self-doubts, and again I couldn't help thinking about how badly I had messed up my life. "I'm honestly not sure if I can ever unconditionally accept myself and my life," I said. That admission made me wonder if my portal journeys would end before I even made it through this one.

"There's someone you want to talk to. It's time to reach out. You will help each other."

6:59.

14

After removing the crust from my eyes, I took a few deep breaths, grabbed my phone from the nightstand and sent the text. "Jean, sorry it's taken me so long to get back to you. I really need to see you."

She replied a couple of hours later, saying that she would see me at 9, after her last patient that night.

When I got to the office, Karine told me that Eric had called to set up dinner. "He said he's still out west but wanted to make sure he got something on your calendar, so I took care of that. He's really interested, I think. I'd love to know what you're going to tell him."

"I'm sorry, Karine. I really don't know what to do. I'm not sure I will until I meet with him."

"I get it," she said, though I could sense the tension and anticipation in her voice.

* * *

I hopped on the subway and made it to Larry's in time for an early dinner before my appointment. Ginette made a pork roast with some garlic mashed potatoes. She may have had some issues with me, but whenever I joined them for dinner, she would prepare one of my favorite meals.

"This looks fantastic, Ginette. Thank you so much for making this."

She nodded.

"So, give me a college update, team," I said.

"She was accepted," Ginette said as my eyes opened widely in anticipation, "to LaGuardia."

Paula looked at her mother and calmly but firmly stated, "I don't care about that! I'll get into Stonebridge, and that's where I'll go."

"Oh, honey," said Ginette. "I hope you do as well. I'm just being practical. Even if you do get accepted, you know that those scholarships are extremely competitive."

Larry kept eating.

"Why don't you tell us what's happening at work, Scott?" Ginette said, in a not-too-subtle attempt to change the conversation.

"Funny you brought that up. I was going to talk to Larry about something that I need some help with, but I'd be happy to ask all of you for your opinion on it."

"That's a great idea," said Larry, sounding relieved.

"Sure, Uncle Scott. I'd love to help," said Paula.

"Well, it's like this . . ."

I filled them all in on the offer from Concord and his challenge with Damon. I then asked for their votes on the subject.

Larry jumped in first. "Before I give you my thoughts, I'm wondering if you could ever forgive Damon for how he treats you and for the things he's done. Because if you can't, there's no reason to vote."

I thought about that. "Let me ask you something. Did you ever forgive Chris Flaggart?"

"I did, actually, and almost told him so when I saw him last year."

"Wait—last year?" I asked.

"Wow, I was sure I told you. I saw Chris at my school one day last June. Get this, he was interviewing for a position as one of the school counselors. Ironic, huh? He'd been selling insurance for years and had gone back to school to get his MSW. He interviewed really well, but some of the people on the hiring committee believed he didn't dress professionally enough. I thought that was ridiculous, and believe it or not, I found myself advocating on his behalf. I was outnumbered, though, and we ended up going with someone else. Kind of a shame for him."

"No, you didn't tell me about that! A counselor, huh? Who'd have thought that? Wonder what he's doing now? I said.

"I'm pretty sure he's still selling insurance. Probably making at least as much as the counselor job, so it all worked out, at least financially," Larry stated.

"So—you said you forgave him. How could you not blame him for what he did?" I asked.

"I never told you this, but I asked myself that same question for years until it dawned on me. As brutal as Chris's act was, I felt that he must have just learned to be like that from his parents, or someone else, and that he, like me, was just acting out of trained conditioning. I'm sure he believed he chose to do what he did, but I don't think so. It was inevitable. What I did was inevitable too, as I struck out from my own frustration and experience because of how I had been bullied. Not by Chris, but by all those who ignored me because my skin color was a few shades darker than theirs. I know this is going to sound really weird, but I didn't feel any different than Chris. I can't judge him when my behavior was just as unacceptable. I'm not saying what he did was a good thing, but it was probably normal for him to do it. I think it's important to tell you that my feeling that way about Chris helped me cope with what I did, too. If it was normal for him, then it was normal for me. But of course, I learned from it, and I know he did as well."

At that moment, I stared into Larry's eyes, trying to detect the beggar. Perhaps Larry had discussed ideas like this with me before, but I didn't recall that he ever had. Maybe he had, and I just didn't hear him. Most likely, though, I heard him but couldn't relate and so, it went over my head. One thing was for sure though: I was in the presence of someone whom I aspired to be more like.

We were all silent until Paula said, "That's crazy shit, Dad," which got a synchronized burst of laughter, head turns, and eyebrow raises from the rest of us.

Larry cast the first vote. "I say give him another chance. You can always leave later."

Ginette followed: "I don't think Damon will ever change. Why not start a new life?"

"Well, there's a tie. What about you, Paula?"

Suddenly, I felt myself slip into a dream-like state. Paula spoke, but no one but me seemed to hear her.

"Once you see yourself in others, you resolve all conflict," she whispered.

"What did you say, Paula?"

"I said I'm sure whatever decision you make, it'll be the best one, Uncle Scott."

* * *

"Your request for a session sounded urgent. Is everything okay?" asked Jean, after I made myself comfortable in her office recliner.

"I really want to be more accepting of myself and others, and I think you can help me with that."

"That's a wonderful thing to work on, but we should also continue the exploration into your past trauma."

"I will do that, Jean. I promise. I just need to learn acceptance."

"Need to, as in that's the urgency? Tell me more about that."

I talked to Jean about how I felt I'd judged everything and everyone in my life, and more than I thought I did. We had a good conversation about that, but then I slipped when she asked me about my goal of nonjudgment and acceptance. Instead of saying something relevant to the two, I blurted out that I couldn't move further in my journey without that.

"I hope the journey you speak of is not related to your dreams," she said sternly.

"Well . . . I really think they're valuable, Jean. In fact, I've gotten a lot of profound information from them so far, and it has definitely had an effect on me."

"And you think that information came from a source other than your own mind?"

I didn't respond.

"Isn't it likely that you already knew those things and had just forgotten that you knew?"

"I don't know," I said, starting to question myself again.

"Scott, this fantasy of yours could cause you to lose your mind. What will it take for you to let the dream thing go?"

"I don't want to let it go."

"What if I can prove you wrong? Will you let it go, then?"

"Prove me wrong? How could you do that?"

"Before I explain it, please answer me. If I can prove you wrong about the reality of these dreams, will you let them go so that we can get to work?"

"I guess if you can *prove* it to me, I'd . . . have to."

"Great. Thank you for having an open mind and know that I appreciate it. You believe the information you get is coming from somewhere other than your mind. Okay then, tonight, in your dreams, ask what my favorite food and color are. And before you think you can just look it up online, know that I don't use social media at all. I will call you tomorrow morning at 9 a.m. to get your answers."

I guess she figured that I'd need to be the world's best detective to find that information out in such a short period of time.

"And what happens if I give you the correct answer?" I asked, thinking that, based on how I had learned what I did about Eric, details about Jean's life might be attainable as well.

"Well then, in that case, I will give you free therapy sessions for a year," she said, confidently. "Although if you give me those answers, I'll be the one who needs therapy."

* * *

Jean's call came in exactly on time. "Hello, Scott. What information do you have for me?" she asked.

"Your favorite color is teal blue," I said, "and your favorite food is coconut cream pie. If someone ever invented a teal-colored coconut cream pie, you'd be in heaven," I said playfully, expecting a laugh. The phone was silent for almost half a minute, which felt like half a century.

"I don't know what to say," she said, in a disappointed tone. "I don't know who you called or what you did, but I know you didn't get this information in your dreams. This doesn't sit well with me. So, we're done, Scott. I will no longer work with you."

Jean hung up. I immediately called her back.

"What do you want?" she said, impatiently.

"Before we part ways, I have a message for you. When you were five years old, you had a puppy named Cobbler."

She was silent.

"My message is that you were just a naïve young girl who made an impulsive and poor decision. You didn't know what you were doing, and at that age, you really couldn't have done any better with your level of consciousness and experience."

She remained silent.

"I am here today to tell you that it is time for forgiveness and acceptance, Jean. That is, it is time for you to forgive yourself. That will stop your nightmares."

I waited through the silence.

"Never contact me again, you son of bitch," she said before she hung up on me again.

15

I spent the next several dreams with the nurse, revisiting various challenging phases of my life, mostly from my teens and twenties. These were times when I felt as if I'd made a mistake and had some regrets about my actions. Each time I judged something, the nurse asked me to first accept that I judged it and then to release that judgment by recognizing the normalcy of how I had acted at the time. The nurse explained that we all do the best we can at all times, all the time. No exceptions. Even if we are ignorant at the time, ignorance does only what ignorance can do, and accepting that as normal was the first step to peace. She didn't suggest that we shouldn't be responsible for our actions, only that based on our level of consciousness, those actions were all normal. That idea really challenged me, but I did believe it was reasonable and actually sounded a lot like what Larry had said about Chris. I also began to believe that with some time and effort, I could actually come to accept myself.

In the middle of one conversation with the nurse, I took a deep breath and said, "You said that you'd help me experience Acceptance when I was better prepared. I'd like to do that now."

"As you wish. I do want to warn you, though, that when you feel Unconditional Acceptance, it might be overwhelming."

I nodded in approval. We were back at the war tent. I saw bombers even closer than before, flying through smoke-filled skies. There were screams coming from the medical tent, and there was blood everywhere. It was still dreadful.

"I don't understand. How is this Acceptance?"

"You will want to experience it through my eyes," she prompted.

I knew what she was suggesting, and as I'd done with the gull and crab, I imagined that I was her. Immediately, I felt the powerful Essence of the beggar again. It was even deeper and more beautiful than the first time I'd experienced it in the city. In my rapture, dream or not, I was again home.

I looked around and saw everything exactly as I saw it all before, but it felt different. It felt like a surreal dream. Instead of disgust, I felt a sense of awe and fascination. I closed my eyes and even more deeply felt the Essence within her—within me. It was perfect. Complete perfection.

I don't know if I was "there" for a few seconds or hours, but when I emerged, I wiped the tears of joy that began to form and lay back on the ground.

"How long was I in that state?" I asked.

"You have always been there and always will be, remember?" she asked.

"Yes, I mean . . . I think I do. Like before, you . . . this . . . feels brand new to me and, at the same time, like something I've always known."

"Tell me about your experience."

"It was overwhelming, but in an amazing way. There was something very strange as well. Instead of wanting everything to go away, I wanted to experience more of it. It wasn't a thought, but a feeling that I wanted it to be brought to me, as if I welcomed it with open arms.

"There were times in my life when I'd experienced such a wanting, but only in regard to pleasant or positive things that could happen. But to have such a desire to experience absolutely anything, even things I'd always judged as horrible—well, that's something I'd never expected to feel.

"There was no judgment of anything, not even of the feelings of awe and fascination I felt. It wasn't until after I came out of that experience that I thought about how wonderful it all was, which then brought the tears. In the experience itself, I was primal, like the gull and crab, operating on instinct."

I paused, reveling in the recall of that feeling. "How can I experience the awe of Acceptance without your help?"

"First, practice nonjudgment, simply by being aware of the judgments you make. Do not be too harsh on yourself for judging; it is normal. But by becoming more aware of your judgments, you will be able to lessen them and eventually prevent them. When you begin to feel less judgmental, remember the idea of bringing life on, meaning, do not just accept what happens, but actually look forward to any experience, even a truly painful one. Just welcome it all and be grateful to be able to have such experiences. Like you said, experience life open-armed, with a sense of joy."

"Wow, that seems like a real challenge, but I'll do my best."

"You always do. Remember that. How would you now describe Acceptance?"

"If Awareness is seeing what is, then Acceptance is the surrendering of judgment around what is seen. It is the unconditionally loving perfection of the Universe. It is actually embracing everything, absolutely, with an unbridled passion for any and all experiences, regardless of how we would judge them with our minds."

"I will see you soon, Scott."

"Wait, what about the key to the next portal?"

"It is a wonderful description that you shared just now. When you wear it as your own, you will have the key."

16

The meeting with Eric was coming up in two days. I sat in my office, debating what would certainly be one of the most important decisions of my career and life. Financial realization versus self-realization, perhaps. The implications, either way, could be enormous.

I wondered if accepting Eric's alluring offer might mean the end of my journey through the portals. I also thought about the nurse's comment about "wearing" acceptance and wondered if it meant embracing Damon for who he was and thus staying with the firm. It felt as if there was a blank sign above my head and my next move would determine what it said.

Karine walked by my front door, and I called her in. I asked her to close the door and have a seat. She did so quietly and waited for me to speak. "I have to say, this is one of the hardest decisions I've ever had to make. Eric presented an amazing opportunity to us. I think you know how much I care about you and that I consider you to be my friend. I hope you know that nothing would make me happier than to see you get all that you deserve. I'm also not a fool, and I would love to reap the rewards of the opportunity for myself.

"The thing is, Damon is a friend too. We've got a lot of history together, and I know that deep down, he's a lot like me, just a lost little boy wanting to be loved. Accepting him would be a big opportunity for me as well.

"I don't know what I should or will do. I guess I just wanted to let you know that either way it goes, I really hope you'll be okay with the decision."

After contemplating all of that, she hugged me without saying a word.

* * *

I arrived early for my dinner with Eric, so I wandered around the cobblestoned streets of SoHo for about a half hour, poking my head into a couple of galleries and doing a little window-shopping. Eric's restaurant was called Ann's Bistro, which he told me was named after a dear friend of his. It was an unassuming place that perfectly reflected his flair for the nondramatic. I didn't know whether the food was extraordinary or if the reputation was the draw, but even in the middle of the week there was a line that went out the front door.

Feeling a little guilty for not having to wait like the others, I was immediately escorted to Eric's table, where his bear hug greeting squeezed the guilt out of me.

"How are you, buddy? Great to see you," he said.

"I'm alive. That feels good to me." It was the first time I'd remembered ever having such a thought. "How was the trip?"

"It was fantastic!" he said. "Signed a new movie deal and spent some time with my costar. When we get a chance, I'd like you to meet her. She's looking to buy some property in the city. Her name is Rose."

"*The* Rose?" I asked, suspecting that he was referring to his frequent movie costar. She was an acclaimed superstar in her own right, with an Oscar to her credits. I'm sure Rose had a last name, but no one ever referred to her other than by the moniker, "The Rose."

"Yeah. *The* Rose," he said, teasingly. "She's really special . . . just like everyone else. And speaking of special, I hope you don't mind that I ordered one of my favorite bottles of wine for us: *Going Forward* Pinot Noir." He paused. "It's my friend's brand," he said, which made me consider just how important close relationships and commitment were to him.

"Sounds great," I said, as we clinked our glasses together.

Between sips of wine, we caught each other up on a few trivial events of the past few weeks, after which he raised the pressing matter at hand. "I assume you've got an answer for me?"

I took another sip of wine, trying to clear my mind. I still had no idea what I was going to say so I bought myself some time. "Let me repeat what I said before; that regardless of what happens, I would love to continue to enjoy our friendship."

"Agreed," he said, without wasting a second.

I took one more sip, put the glass down, looked him in the eye and took a deep breath.

"I have decided to stay at the firm and give it another try with Damon. It's not about my owing him anything; it's more for me than him. I'd like to try to accept him for who he is, and in the process, I hope to see myself as more of who I'd like to become. We're all on a journey, and I think accepting him is part of mine. But that's my journey, Eric, not yours, and I don't expect you to accept him at all. I just want you to understand that my decision is really about me, not about Damon, and certainly in no way a reflection of how I feel about you. I've made my decision, and I'm prepared to live with yours."

He sat back in his chair, pursed his lips, tilted his head, and looked up to consider what I'd said. I didn't think my statement shocked him, but I did think he was hoping for a different one.

As he sat silently, my mind became very still as well. I had no desires, no attachment to any particular outcome, no thoughts at all. My future was unknown, but the moment wasn't. I recognized it from the street in New York. I felt a sense of peace that warmed my body and once more gave me a brief taste of what could only have been heaven.

I barely noticed a young waiter, dressed in nicely pressed jeans and a black shirt, pacing around our table like a young man in a delivery room waiting for his first child.

"Hey, Willy. It's okay, you can take our orders."

"I'm sorry, sir. I prefer not to intrude on people when they are engaged in deep conversation."

"How many times have I asked you not to call me sir?" Eric asked, with an obvious touch of humor.

"Sorry, sir . . . I mean, sorry." We all laughed.

"What can I get for you?"

"Please ask Elizabeth what she recommends tonight."

"Very good, sir . . . Damn it!"

Even a few people from the tables near us laughed.

"Willy, I'd like you to meet my new business partner. This is Scott Billings."

"Hello, Mr. Billings," the young man said.

Still in a beautiful daze, I heard myself say "I'll have whatever the chef recommends, as well. Thanks, Willy, and nice to meet you."

After Willy left the table it took a few more moments before I could focus. "Are you sure that's what you want, Eric?"

"No, that's not exactly what I want. But I still get *who* I want."

"Thanks for saying that."

"I do have to say something else, though. If Damon causes any challenges, I will have no choice but to pull the account, and very quickly. Also, I want you and Karine to handle all of our transactions. I hope you understand and can do that."

"I absolutely understand, and we will. Thank you, Eric."

Eric poured another glass of wine for us and looked me in the eye before saying, "You're welcome, partner."

17

The third portal was nearly illuminated to its max but not ready for me to enter, as I still hadn't found the key. Instead, I started thinking about the bonus check I'd soon get and decided to fly over Manhattan to see what areas attracted my attention as possible places to live. I explored a few potentially desirable neighborhoods before flying over to Central Park. When I saw the fountain again, I landed to sit on its edge. It was a beautiful, sunny day, and I soaked in the rays, wondering if I'd be tan when I woke up.

I looked around and saw people walking, running, and riding bicycles. Several children ran by, playing a game of tag. I saw a group of people sitting on a brightly colored blanket, engaged in conversation as they ate and drank. Beside the picnickers, a lone man sat on the grass. He was dressed in gray and wore a black baseball cap, and I recognized him immediately and wasted no time in approaching him.

I stood before him and he kept his head down. "What the hell are you looking at?" he asked in a deep and menacing tone.

There it was. That line again. Whatever it meant, this time, I was ready to stand up for myself.

"What do you want from me?" I demanded.

He didn't respond, just continued to sit, head down.

"I said, what do you want!?"

He still didn't respond.

"I'll tell you what I want, then. You will leave me alone. I don't want to see you again. Leave here, now, and stay out of my life!"

I snapped my fingers, and he disappeared. I felt a release and believed I was finally rid of him.

18

I spoke to Karine when I got in the next morning. I suspected that she might have been disappointed, but all she said was, "Let's do it, Scott!" Fortuitously, Damon was standing in the hallway, and we invited him into my office.

"I hope you have good news," Damon said.

"Please sit down." I offered one of the chairs in front of my desk and held my hand out until he sat. Karine sat in the other chair.

"I actually have great news," I said. "First, we have secured the Concord account."

Damon jumped out of his chair to reach for my hand. I reached as well and when they were about to meet, I pulled mine back, then finished with the Phi Five handshake. He laughed, and Karine stared at us with a bewildered smile on her face.

"Wow, forgot about that. Thanks for the reminder. I can't tell you how happy I am to hear about the account. Really. Well done, guys. Okay, what are the next steps?" he asked.

"Well, Concord was pretty clear about something. It will be only Karine and me overseeing his affairs. No one else."

As Damon's pride took hold of him, the celebration ended quickly. "Well, I think you should just tell him that's not the way it works around here."

"With all due respect, boss, that's the way it's going to work."

He looked surprised at my calm resolve and went silent. I took the opportunity to try to read his thoughts, just as I had done with the gull and crab. Perhaps it was just my imagination, but I believed I could actually pick up on the various things he was rattling around in his mind to save his self-image and take back some control over the situation.

I decided to use that information and head him off at the pass. "Eric doesn't know you or what you can do, and even though you and I haven't been as close as we used to be, I still have faith in you. Please have some faith in us. We landed the account, right? Now give Karine and me a chance to make us all some money. Don't worry about a thing, and know that we'll count on your experience whenever we need it. We won't let you down."

Seemingly somewhat relieved by that assurance, he stood up, shook my hand, albeit normally, then walked out of my office.

"Wow, Scott," said Karine, as she nodded in approval and then left my office.

* * *

Over the next few weeks, I worked on the Concord account nonstop. One afternoon, I was deep in research when Karine let me know that I had a visitor.

"Really? There's no one on the schedule, Karine. Did I miss something?"

I couldn't make out the muted conversation between them. "She says her name is Jean, and she would like to speak with you."

"Shit," I whispered. Considering what I'd just experienced with Damon, it was ironic that I felt a quick pang of fear as I believed the little boy in me was about to get scolded. I gained some composure and asked Karine to send her in.

She entered, carrying a small, thin box, and looking like a completely different person than the therapist I knew. She wore very casual yoga pants and a soft, colorful shirt. Her hair was tied up in a youthful ponytail. As she sat down on the chair in front of my desk, I relaxed and walked around my desk to sit next to her.

"I'll bet you're surprised to see me here."

"A little," I confirmed.

"I don't know where to begin," she said. "After that call with you, I was very angry. I thought for sure you somehow dug into my past, and in doing so, invaded my personal life. But after a few days, I realized that I'd never told anyone what happened to the dog. At the time, I just made up a story, and my parents believed it. Also, no one knew I was having nightmares. I've been having them for years."

She leaned forward. "So then, I kept asking myself the same question: What are the implications of you getting that information from your dreams? I have to tell you, the thought of that alone rocked me a little. Well, it rocked me a lot. Once I finally let go of the rational thought that told me what you did was impossible, I felt a sense of peace like I've never felt. A release, of sorts, into a feeling of complete calm. Last night was the first that I could remember in which I didn't have a nightmare."

"That's fantastic, Jean. I'm really happy for you. I know I sounded confident on the phone, but I have to admit that I had, and probably still have, some doubts about the validity of the dreams. Hearing you now really helps me. Thanks. I guess they really are a gift. You are too."

"Well, speaking of gifts . . ." She picked up the box that she had set down on the floor. "I said that I was rocked. So, I thought about how I could thank you and decided to rock your world in return. You asked me how to accept yourself and others, and the thing that came to me was that we are all different and that instead of resisting those differences, accepting them is the key to peace."

She opened the box and pulled out a tee shirt. "Remember when we discussed your influences and you told me you loved music, especially classical and rock, but you didn't particularly enjoy Bruce Springsteen?"

"Hmm, vaguely, a couple years ago, yeah."

"Well, what I didn't tell you was that Bruce is my favorite artist." With that, she handed me the shirt, which portrayed the image of Springsteen and the E Street Band.

"This is a reminder for you, and perhaps more for me, that people should have open minds and not only accept, but embrace, the differences between us all. Please wear this shirt, Scott, and then maybe realize, after all, that we're not so different."

I chuckled to myself, as I didn't realize that the nurse's comment about "wearing acceptance" was literal. I was, however, very happy to now hold the key to the next portal. "Thank you, Jean. So I'll see you every week for the rest of my life . . . at no charge, of course." I grinned.

"Truthfully, if that's what you really wanted, I would be honored. Something tells me that you're going in another direction, though. I do hope I see you again, someday soon."

We hugged goodbye, and I pulled out my notepad to add another entry to my journal.

Uncovering the Truth
Portal 1—Aware is what we can be. Awareness is the way of Being.
Portal 2—Accepting is how we can act. Acceptance is the open arms of the Universe.

19

I neared the third portal and felt the snugness of the Springsteen tee shirt against my chest as I moved. I was amazed at how these dreams sometimes felt more realistic than my waking state. The third portal was now lit up like the first two, and I entered it with an open mind.

I was transported to a classroom in which the chairs were arranged in semicircles facing the front. I chose an empty seat in the back row and slipped into it from the side, as it was the kind with a desk attached to it. The chair brought back memories of my school days, and I wondered briefly how many pieces of gum were stuck to its underside.

I turned my attention to the others in the room as I tried to figure out where I was. The teacher's back was to the class; he was writing something I couldn't see on the whiteboard on the wall.

The casually dressed students looked to be about ten years old. A chart on one of the closet doors entitled "Class 5-3 Rules" confirmed that I was in a fifth-grade classroom. As I continued observing, now looking for clues as to why I was here, the teacher turned back to us, revealing the word "Knowing" on the whiteboard. I was in the Portal of Knowing. I took a closer look at the teacher and it was unmistakably the beggar, but he looked a little like Larry. When he spoke, he sounded a little like Larry as well.

"Today we are continuing our exploration of some of the mysteries of the universe."

The students stirred in anticipation. Seemed like heavy stuff for a fifth-grade class.

"My first question is, what is faith?" he asked the class.

One of the nearly dozen students in the room quickly raised her hand and didn't wait to be called on. "It is the belief in something that cannot be or has not yet been proven."

"Very good, Elyse," he said. "And why would anyone need to believe in something that cannot be known for sure?"

The same girl raised her hand and blurted out, "That is a trick question."

"Oh, really? Why is that, Elyse?"

"Because things can be known for sure, even if they are not proven."

"And how can you know for sure, Elyse?"

"From the mindless experience of it. Only the mind requires proof. Without the interference of your mind, you are the Knowing that permeates the Universe."

Elyse was no ordinary student, I quickly realized.

"Okay, let us hear from someone else for this one." Elyse folded her arms and beamed with confidence as she sat back in her chair, and the teacher continued. "What is the purpose of faith?"

No hands went up. Elyse scanned the room and waited, not so patiently, for someone to respond. The boy who finally did sported deep blue hair. I suspected that, even in the dream world, it wasn't his natural color.

"Faith is a guiding light," he said. "It will eventually lead you to Truth. If you have a philosophy that works for you and a strong confidence and trust in your belief system, then your path to Truth can be hastened."

And apparently, this was no ordinary fifth-grade class.

"Why is that?" asked the teacher.

Elyse and the blue-haired boy both looked around the room, apparently expecting someone else to take over the tag team effort. Another boy from across the room spoke up.

"It's because faith offers clarity in direction. It provides us with a path to figuring things out without all the mind chatter."

"Very good, Sammy," said the teacher. "My next question is a little more challenging. Faith is a powerful tool that we could all use a little more of. It stems from our innate desire to remember the truth. That desire is a naturally occurring process within all of us that eventually leads to Knowing. There are many things in which people have faith, and my question is, even without a lifetime of experience, what is one thing we *all* absolutely and intrinsically know as Truth?"

"What is your answer . . . let me see . . ." he picked up a clipboard from his desk and read from it. "Scott?" Now the entire class turned their heads to stare at me.

"I don't think we can know anything for sure, right?" I said.

The class chuckled.

"I mean, how could we really know anything, really? Isn't it all speculation?"

"Class, please tell Scott what we all know as Truth." They all spoke in unison, as if they were reciting the Pledge of Allegiance.

"I know that I exist. I know I am here. I know that I Am. This I know as Truth."

Elyse continued, "That is what I know; what we *all* know. I might exist as a character in your dream, or we both may be characters in someone else's. I could be just about anything. I might even exist as an illusion. But I know that I exist. We all experience that one same thing as Truth. First, have faith in that idea, and then know it to be Truth, from a place beyond cognition."

By her answer, I understood that she meant that when one is able to still the mind, there is a sense of knowing that exists in the void between thoughts. How I understood that was beyond me.

"Can someone please tell me exactly what the mind is?" I jumped in and asked.

Sammy continued, "You perceive the world through the senses and store all those perceptions as memories within your brain, which catalogs those memories and creates a summary of them. The brain is like a computer in that when it stores those experiences, organizes, and assembles them, it then prints out your picture of reality. And that is all the mind is—a construct of memories that creates your world and self-image. That is also why we are in this portal, because we are helping you change your mind. Even if you change only one thought, your inner computer changes, and so then does your experience of the world."

The teacher jumped in. "Remember this very important point: You are just one idea away from a new reality." He turned and wrote on the whiteboard, "One Idea Away."

"And here's another thing to remember. Because your mind has created a singular viewpoint of reality, it lives within the illusion that what it believes is the *only* reality. Each of us sees *our* world, but we do not see *the* world."

"Perhaps it is from one of the other portals I've visited, but something tells me that what you've shared is the truth. But just when I think I've got it, I feel like I lose it, quickly. On my journey,

I've learned a lot about the ego. Maybe mine is preventing me from getting this?"

Elyse chimed in, "The only thing preventing you from understanding is that you don't remember who you really are. Know also that mind, self, personality, ego . . . all really the same; just different words for the same concept. Words are also, of course, recognized patterns created by our minds. Patterns that keep us limited and separated from our True Self. Focusing too much on words will keep your mind full. You'd prefer to be mind*less*, trust me."

"Thank you, Elyse. One more thing, Scott. The more consciously aware you are, the more able you are to create and manifest what you choose to experience. And part of choosing the reality you desire is having something powerful to base your reality on. So now, class, let's talk about what a working belief system for Scott will look like. Anyone?"

I raised my hand. "I'm sorry if I keep slowing down the class, but what do you mean by working belief system?"

"Do not apologize for wanting to understand," said the teacher. "We are all in search of the truth. Everyone is, whether they realize it or not. The love of Truth creates an amazingly powerful inner pull. One important step in finding the truth is to develop faith in a belief system, which is a collection of ideas you have about the way life works. When a belief system works for you, it brings you toward your True Nature. It works against you if it takes you further from it. You can believe anything you choose, but realize that up until this point in your life, your current beliefs have mostly been chosen for you by others. You really have not been actively involved in that process. Until recently, those beliefs have created a very unhappy and unfulfilling life for you."

"I understand what you're saying. How do I create a belief system that works for me?"

"Before you are ready to do that, you will need to find the foundational idea for all belief systems, the thing that will shift your focus. This one thing will help you consciously choose your beliefs and will act as a yardstick upon which to measure all actions."

"Where do I find that?" I asked.

"From the peculiarities of genius."

"The what?"

6:59.

20

I stood and waved to Nowell as he entered Las Puertas. He was wearing the same outfit he wore each day at work, including his signature suspenders.

"Nice to have you join me here, Nowell. I'm sorry we haven't had a chance to connect personally before this."

"Hi, Mr. Billings. Thanks for inviting me."

Ava greeted Nowell in Spanish, and I sat, amazed, as the two of them had what seemed like a very pleasant exchange. Nowell spoke Spanish with a highly unanticipated fluency. It sounded quite beautiful.

She recommended the chef's special, *camerones en cerveza*. "It's delicious."

Different had definitely been on the menu recently, so I asked if it would be possible for the chef to come out and explain the dish to us.

"Oh, I'm sorry, *compañero*," she said. "He's very shy and prefers to stay in his station."

I tried to look back into the kitchen to see if I could catch a glimpse of him. He must truly have been shy, as I didn't remember ever having seen him. Nowell ordered for us in Spanish. I wasn't sure what was ordered for me, but I had other things on my mind and waited until Ava walked away.

I first asked Nowell the meaning of the greeting. He said it meant "partner." I thought that was a very nice way to greet customers, but I didn't feel much like a partner, as I barely remembered her name and actually knew little to nothing about Las Puertas.

"Nowell, what do you know about this place? Why isn't it ever busy? Who is the chef?"

He looked a little confused. I wondered if I had just challenged him to break confidences. He turned to see Ava still nearby. She nodded at him, and he began to answer.

"Señora Ava and her son, Lennon, the chef, have owned this place for several years. They built the business themselves."

In that moment, everything I had surmised about Las Puertas was turned upside down. I had no idea that Ava was the owner or that she had a son or that he was the chef. It was only then that I realized I'd never seen anyone other than Ava working in the restaurant.

"Señora Ava lost her husband years ago. He left her enough money to come to New York and open this place. It was her dream," he continued, in a sad tone.

"What's wrong, Nowell?"

"They are going to have to close soon. There are just not enough customers coming in, and they do not have the money to advertise."

"Oh no!" I exclaimed. "That's horrible. I love this place. Ava is so nice to people, and the food is excellent. I don't know what to say."

"Wait here, please," said Nowell. He got up and walked into the kitchen, returning a few minutes later with a young man who couldn't have been more than twenty-five.

"This is Mr. Billings, Lennon."

"Hello, sir," he said, softly.

"Hello, Lennon. How are you doing?"

"Oh, I'm okay, sir. I'm making something wonderful tonight," he said, proudly. "You will love it."

I pried a bit to follow up on a hunch.

"Where do you live, Lennon?"

Lennon looked at Nowell, who nodded encouragingly.

"I live here, sir, in the back, with my mom. I need to get back to the cooking. Nice meeting you, sir."

"They really live here?"

"Yes," said Nowell.

I thought it ironic that I had been exploring a portal that dealt with belief systems and part of mine had just been shaken beyond belief. I replayed mental images of many visits to the restaurant, wondering if it was ever busy, if I tipped enough, or if I'd recommended the place enough. *How could I not have realized what was really going on here? How could I have missed so much?*

"Thank you, Ava," I said when she brought our drinks. I don't think I'd ever addressed her by her name. She smiled my way. I then realized that I had missed something else. She was a very beautiful woman.

I turned my attention back too Nowell. "Do you mind if I ask you a very personal question, Nowell?"

"I do not."

"I'm wondering about your clothing. Do you have anything other than that to wear?"

"I do. A lot of clothing. I just feel like myself when I wear this. Does it offend you?"

"No, of course not. In fact . . . you're right; it is you."

I looked more closely at him, now wondering if he really was who he appeared to be. It was almost a moot point though, as lately no one appeared to be as I'd seen them before the dreams began. It occurred to me that perhaps I was sensing a part of the beggar within each person I encountered.

"Would you mind telling me your thoughts on belief systems?" I said, changing the subject.

Nowell talked for about twenty minutes straight, not even pausing when the main course arrived. Apparently, I had dialed into a comfortable topic for him. He explained how he had learned that our belief systems are formed when we are very young and impressionable, then for the rest of our lives, our egos look in whichever direction reinforces those beliefs.

He told me that people are very protective of what they believe in, that they are often ready and willing to fight, sometimes even kill or die, rather than admit or even consider that they aren't very sure of what they believe or why they believe in whatever they do.

"Even when people feel something is off with one of their ideas," he continued, "I mean, when they hear their intuition tell them so, most just ignore it. I think they do that partly because they are afraid of being wrong and therefore appearing ignorant or vulnerable. Pride can hold a lot of people back. The biggest block, I think, is that most people identify and define themselves from within their self-created projections and cannot handle any challenge to the foundation of their world. If they lose their self-created image, they believe they will lose their entire sense of being; their entire self."

For the life of me, I couldn't comprehend how I had never spoken with Nowell before. I made so many assumptions about him, never realizing what a deep and insightful person he was. Yes, he was a little different, but he was also amazing. I understood why Karine liked him so much.

The meal was truly marvelous. It occurred to me how much I'd been missing by never ordering anything other than my favorite dish. Creatures of habit, we are. So much potential, and yet, so limited in realizing that potential.

"May I ask what it is that you believe in, Nowell?"

"I believe in loving-kindness. I think people should love themselves, love others, love nature, love everything. When I think, feel, or act, I try to do so in a kind way." He stopped for a moment to consider something and then continued with a sense of conviction. "That's the most important thing I believe in. If you're looking to explore your beliefs, Mr. Billings, I'd highly recommend that as a foundation. You can't go wrong with kindness."

"Please call me Scott, Nowell."

"Thank you, sir, but I'd prefer Mr. Billings if that's okay with you."

He really *was* weird, but in a very, very cool way.

"Where did you get all those ideas, Nowell?"

"Just one of my peculiarities I guess, Mr. Billings."

I paused for a moment, now realizing that my teachers were everywhere.

"Well, Nowell. I think you're a genius. A very wise and peculiar genius."

21

I was back in class, and everyone was standing.

"Remember to stay close together and keep connected with a buddy. Pair up now." The class scattered around the room to find a partner. Elyse walked directly to me.

"How about you and me?"

"Sure, Elyse. That would be nice."

"You know how it's done, everyone. Hold each other's hands." The teacher waited until all pairs were connected. "Okay, class. Scott needs some new ideas to rework his belief system. We will help him, just as we did with each of you."

The teacher snapped his fingers, and we were in deep space, all of us, just floating around holding hands. There were bright stars everywhere. It was truly a spectacle to behold. It was the blue-haired boy who began my orientation.

"A belief system is something either you create or, if you do not, is created for you. It is influenced by every experience you have had, but you can change it in an instant. Going back to the computer analogy, your beliefs create the program that runs on your operating system. That program is your life. In order to re-create that program, you can simply choose a new program, anything you would like, one small rewrite at a time."

Elyse took over. "Anything at all. With one stipulation. If you want that belief system to work for you and bring you happiness, all of your beliefs will have to be checked and measured against one simple principle. This principle needs to be first, above all others. It needs to be a principle that is associated with a high level of consciousness, something that resonates closely with Truth. Without it, chaos ensues, and you will continue to struggle. Have you figured out what that principle is yet?"

"It is the belief that whatever I choose to think, feel, or do," I replied, "must include loving-kindness to everything and everyone, including me."

"That's it!" said the teacher. "If you keep loving-kindness as a guide, it will help you release suffering and move you closer to your True Nature. That's because loving-kindness *is* closer to your True Nature."

"Yes, I can see how that can be."

I continued to enjoy the beauty of the stars. They began to pulse in and out—they were all there one second and then they were all gone. Then suddenly, after one of the pulses, they remained invisible, replaced by a vast darkness, a pitch-black void, except for one tiny point of light, almost imperceptible to my eyes. The energy was intensifying. I'd never felt anything that powerful before. This seemed like the big bang, but different from what I'd learned about it because I could feel a vibration of energy all around me, even in the darkened void. I always thought the big bang was the thing that actually created energy.

Then it happened. From that tiny point came an explosion that was louder and hotter than anything I could have ever imagined. It produced a brilliant light that lit up the entire universe in all directions, for as far as I could see.

The teacher's voice interrupted my awestruck observation, asking "What are you choosing to believe about that event?"

"I felt energy around us increasing before the explosion, and it must have come from somewhere. I think maybe God. I don't know. But I'd love to know the truth."

"Scott," said the teacher, "you have beliefs about everything. Some work for you, and those are the ones you want to cultivate. Some beliefs work against you, and those are the kind you want to change. And some beliefs simply do not matter. You need to learn the differences between them all. That way, you can focus your energy on the things that *do* matter to you. There are so many thoughts that can distract you. Focusing on the ones that really matter will improve your life experience more quickly. We started here in space because you hold the belief that the big bang created the universe. This is the type of belief that does not matter. As long as you are comfortable with it, you can just accept it and leave it be."

"Why doesn't the truth about the origin of the universe matter?" I asked.

"It does not matter because even if you knew the truth about it, it would not change your life. You will dramatically change your life if you remember who you really are, why you are here, and how to live a happy, fully engaged existence. It is not necessary to know the answer to every question. It is a fine and healthy quality to be curious, but *needing* to know is the ego wanting to exert a sense of control over everything. The ego's need depletes your energy and focus. Sometimes it is enlightening to just embrace some of the mysteries of life.

"If you are happy with your beliefs that the big bang created the universe and that perhaps it was God who caused the big bang to happen, and if believing those things does no harm to anyone, then believe them. One thing that is very important that I should mention here is that your belief system belongs to you. There's no harm in sharing it with people who are interested, but it is not lovingly kind to force your ideas onto those who may not be interested. People who force their beliefs onto others do so to try to control them. This usually stems from a weak sense of self and a lack of faith in their own beliefs."

I considered that and realized how often I got into arguments when people tried to push their ideas on me. I thought about what the nurse had taught me in the second portal about conflict; that it derives from a feeling of being separate. The thought then came to me that it takes two separate people to create a conflict and that I didn't need to be one of them.

I looked around the classroom, and a strange but appropriate idea popped into my head. "You know, it occurs to me that the nature of conflict really comes down to shoes, or more specifically, people's reluctance to try on any pair besides their own. That's what happens when people fight over religion or politics. So, speaking of religion, what should I have faith in with regard to that path?"

"Very appropriate choice of words, as there are many paths to take, all leading to the same place," said the teacher.

With that, one of the smallest students, a child prodigy I imagined, a cute girl with pigtails, spoke out for the first time. "Like bowling with bumpers on!" she exclaimed. Everyone laughed along with her.

The teacher continued. "Whether it is through religion, an inner voice, or the guidance of teachers, each of us must find our own path to Knowing, which is the essential understanding of all things. Religion is a vehicle that works for many people, but follow whatever path you feel will help you remember the truth."

"I want the path that takes me to what I've recently felt. That indescribable experience of bliss. I think that is the truth, but how will I really even know what Truth is?"

Elyse spoke up: "The illusion ends when everything that is not Truth fades from your reality. Have faith in that, too."

"In the meantime, listen to the voice of loving-kindness," said the blue-haired boy. "You already know this inner voice; it is your true voice."

"May I ask, who am I, really?"

"You are not yet ready to let your mind go. Please ask that question when you know you are ready," remarked the teacher.

"So in the meantime, I suppose I have to just keep questioning everything, kind of a trial-and-error process?"

"Yes, you will continually question and discern between the temporary, limited fantasies that your mind creates and the Knowing that is unlimited and permanent. It is a process of *uncovery*, that is, uncovering the truth from all that it is not. This is what all awakening people do, and we call it . . . class?"

They all spoke in unison. "True versus Truth."

"True is what you think you know; it's what you believe with your limited, finite, and logical mind," added Elyse. "All things that are true are true for an individual or even a group of them. Those meanderings have no permanence to them. Truth is Knowing—that which does not change. Its permanent nature can be intuitively felt within every soul in the world, but only when we surrender the control of our minds. Truth is beyond limitation, separation, or individuation.

"As another guide to distinguish between true and Truth, remember that any idea that separates you, limits you, or attempts to define you in any way is an idea that moves you further from Truth. The people, places, things, and ideas that unite you are those that move you closer to your True Essence."

"Good job, class. Yes, to eventually know the truth, you have to learn to distinguish it from what your mind believes is true." The teacher pointed to the small pigtailed girl. "She had the right idea. Don't try too hard to figure out the truth right now. Instead, just get on a path to recognize what you think *might* be truth and start there. Just make sure you write down your ideas in pencil instead of pen."

"And how do I even begin to choose beliefs that will work for me?"

"I am glad you asked, as that is a most important part of this journey. To learn to discern Truth from true, you need to at least have an initial idea, even if it's just a guess, of what the truth is. One way to think about Knowing is to relate it to *intuition*. Your intuition will help you. Listen carefully to it. Until you can distinguish intuition from self-created thought, you will need to continually test and refine what comes to you. But use whatever current version of what you think is truth as a working definition until you replace it. You might continually replace it all your life, but each time will move you closer to your True Nature."

"I'm not sure how to listen to my intuition."

"Intuition comes in many forms. You've been experiencing yours through various forms of chills and feelings. You have also resonated with concepts that just felt correct to you. Additionally, you have just known some things and have questioned how you knew them. You didn't even understand or necessarily agree with what came to you. All of that is your intuition speaking to you. Keep refining yours, as it is your way of providing you with directional signs to Truth.

"Consider what you have experienced in this portal and the others. What has your intuition told you about the nature of Truth, and how do you relate to that information? Remember, your answer should feel like it comes not from your mind but from a place, an intelligence, beyond logic or reason."

"The thing that has rung most true so far is that there is a conscious universe, creating all I see. With that thought, I can see all that is before me, without my filters, which allows me to experience more of what the world offers. Also, the idea of Consciousness being unconditionally accepting is very peaceful, and my being more accepting of myself will help me rest a little easier, even when I think I screw up a bit. Speaking of which, I believe nonjudgment is the only way Consciousness can be, so that is a goal that will always be a work in progress for me. Loving-kindness is a great sounding board for how to treat myself and others. Besides the obvious, is also means appreciating every person or experience for what it can offer. I also relate to the idea of an intelligent universe, one that I can connect to when I quiet my mind.

"All those ideas resonate within me, perfectly. As you requested, I will continue to question everything with a curious and open mind, but I do believe those things are the truth. I've felt them to be so. That is the same feeling I had when I first met you on the sidewalk."

It occurred to me that so far, in all his incarnations and even when I referenced our first encounter, the beggar never revealed to me who he really was, though he didn't make any attempt to hide or deny it either.

"That is a wonderful start," said the teacher. "So while you keep refining those concepts, remember to measure any thoughts, feelings, and actions against those resonating ideas. If anything you think, feel, or do better connects you to those concepts, then you can trust that you are on the right track. If anything pulls you away from those concepts, then you will be moving away from Truth. That path will take you from what you think you know, to pure Knowing."

"I actually think I've been doing that since I first stumbled upon the dream world."

"You have. Although I doubt it was a stumble," said the teacher. "Now just trust that it will take you where you truly yearn to go.

Remember that you don't have to try very hard. In fact, you do not have to try at all. If anything, let go of trying, just release. As you release your preconceived notions, the truth will be revealed."

"Like the statue whose true nature is uncovered only when the outer layers are removed," said the pigtailed girl, which earned her a few hugs from the others.

The teacher jumped in: "Yes, chip away at your statue, Scott."

"In the meantime," said Elyse, "why not use your mind in the way it's designed? The mind's purpose—and it achieves it wonderfully—is to allow you to experience life in your own unique way. Tap into the creative genius of yours and manifest the world you want to experience. That way, you can turn your dreams into reality."

"We live in the world of possibility," said Sammy. That struck a chord, as I remembered Karine using similar words. "Choose and create your experience. That's where your power lies, in the ability to choose your reality. Once you truly understand this power, you are more likely to understand your nature as both creation and Creator."

"Wait a minute," I said, curiously, challenging not them as much as my past beliefs. "How can I be sure that the idea of creating my own reality isn't just an act of self-deception? I mean, what about the real world, filled with pain and suffering, and the restrictions imposed on people by genetics or by other people, based on race, color, or physical limitations? How do I bridge the gap between the world I see and the reality I have now felt?"

With that, a loud whistle, along with the unmistakable sound of an approaching diesel engine, turned our heads in the direction of the oncoming train. Though it had sounded much bigger, when it pulled up, I saw that it was just a single locomotive train car. It slowed to a stop, and we all boarded.

"Why don't we just project ourselves to where we want to go?" I asked.

"In anticipation of the destination, it is more often than not that our journeys are not appreciated. We could all use a little more enjoyment of the ride," said the teacher. I sat back, trying to enjoy that one.

I felt the train slowing as we reached a small town. We stopped, and when we got off, many small children ran past us. Several adults behind them were walking more slowly in the same direction.

The pigtailed girl and the blue-haired boy each held one of my hands and began pulling me to follow all the others. And there were many others. When we arrived at our destination, I was surprised to see what was most likely the entire population of the town staring at the front porch of a small log cabin. On it, a white-haired woman dressed in a pretty pink dress and a matching bonnet on her head rocked back and forth and appeared to be knitting, though I was too far away to tell for sure. People sat very quietly all around the porch and yard surrounding the cabin, watching the woman.

"Who is she?" I asked.

"Shhhhh," replied the blue-haired boy.

The woman briefly looked up. I eagerly waited to hear what I expected to be wisdom of the ages. I waited and continued waiting. She looked very content and peaceful but said nothing for what seemed like forever. I looked around to see if others lost focus, but none appeared to. They all looked enchanted with the woman.

The day turned into night and nothing changed. Not a peep from the crowd nor a word from the woman. I finally closed my eyes, and when I did, I began to feel something. Something beautiful. I felt solid on the ground and at the same time like I was floating. It seemed like my entire body was vibrating, rapidly. Only a few distracting thoughts popped in here and there, but even those quickly faded. Everything made sense.

It must have been the middle of the night when the woman stood from her rocking chair, grabbed whatever she was working on, turned around, and walked into the log cabin. Everyone then arose and began walking away from the cabin. When I looked more closely, I could tell that everyone, including me, had a slight glow to them, similar to the one I saw on the first portal before it lit up in full force.

"What do you know?" asked the teacher as we walked back toward the train.

"I don't know what to think."

"Yes, don't think," he said. "Thinking is like trying to feel with your mind. Know with your Essence instead. You were doing that before in front of the cabin. Your intuition was speaking. You were listening without your mind and hearing without attaching any labels, judgments, or thoughts onto what you heard. You already know the answer to my question. You know all answers. Now, what do you know?"

The pigtailed girl put a flower in my hand, and I felt a comforting chill and a sense of being grounded and free that resonated though my entire body, the same things I'd felt with my eyes closed by the cabin and on the sidewalk in New York. I was not *trying* to know; I just knew. In that mindless moment, I understood that Knowing was something to which I always had access and that the voice that spoke to me is the same voice that speaks to all humans, animals, plants—everything. I recognized then that the voice had always been there, but I'd been so busy thinking that I hadn't heard it.

"I don't have to figure out, understand, or even agree with what happens in the world, as none of that changes the reality of what is, a reality that I'm just beginning to see." I took my usual deep cleansing breath. "I am Knowing; that is all there is to know," I said.

"Why do you believe the woman remained silent?"

"She shared her wisdom by sharing her Essence. By being. There was nothing that needed to be said. Knowing is not of the mind and cannot be understood through the spoken word. It is a shared sense of Truth that resonates within each of us, within all of us."

"Yes, we came here because you asked about the reality of living in your world, Scott," said the teacher. "You doubted the idea that you can create a world of your choosing by altering your belief system, because you thought that some part of you was at the effect of the cruelties of the world. What do you think of those doubts now?"

"Even though only a few times and just very briefly, I've tasted reality in very sacred and heavenly moments. In those moments, I am everywhere and there is only Knowing. I guess the purpose of this trip is to remind myself that no matter what beliefs I have about the world, it is still just the mind's dream, and that when I am Knowing, all the human drama fades and nothing is unknown."

"You *guess* that?" asked Elyse.

"I know it," I said, "but I'm still unsure about what to do in my waking state. If what I think isn't real, why has all the suffering I've experienced been so devastatingly painful?"

"The human mind thinks it is real," Elyse replied. "It believes it is an entity unto itself, which is why it is also referred to as the 'self.' Because your individual mind does not remember its connection to the One Mind, you believe you live in a world of isolation, separation, and limitation, an illusion which causes you to suffer. People get confused by the word illusion," Elyse went on. "It simply means that we do not see the world as it actually is but instead see it with the filters of the mind. Just because something is an illusion it doesn't mean you should ignore it. Whether something actually exists or not is irrelevant, because you are having a real experience with it. So yes, until there is no longer suffering and drama, you do need to learn how to handle it. Raise your consciousness not only by remembering that you're connected to the One Mind, but by knowing that you *are* the One Mind. Feel it as your Essence. Know it as Truth. Do this and you will never again suffer."

That reminded me of what the nurse and I had discussed about pain and acceptance. Not sure if I was completely getting the concept, I asked, "You mean I can get to the point where things 'just are,' and I won't feel the need to change anything?"

With that, the teacher snapped his fingers, and we were once again on the train. "One more stop for you," he said.

We stopped in a desert-like area in which I could only see a single tent. There were a few people holding open the flap at the tent's entryway. By the way they were dressed, I figured that we were somewhere in India.

A heavily robed man slowly walked toward the tent, his elbows supported by the guiding hands of two young men. I'd gotten pretty good at sensing other's experiences since I'd first tried it with the gull and crab, so I cleared my mind and imagined I was him. Within seconds, I felt a pain that was almost too much for me to bear. I watched as he entered the tent, took off his robe, and sat down and closed his eyes. Almost immediately, the pain was gone, leaving only peace. I relaxed and continued to feel a sense of peace as I watched him meditate. When he was finished, he put the robe, along with the pain, back on. At that point, his agony was unbearable, and I stepped outside, coming back into my own body.

I stopped him as he walked out of the tent. "I'm very sorry to intrude, but would you mind if I asked you a question?"

"I am here for you," was his response.

"You have the amazing ability to remove your pain when you choose to, so why take it back on and suffer?"

"There is pain, but there is no suffering," he said.

I stood for a few moments, watching him hobble away as I absorbed his words. If I could truly believe the lesson I'd just learned and figure out how to incorporate it in my life, I was sure that my entire experience of the world would be forever changed.

I blinked, and we were back in the classroom.

"I think we all had a great trip, right?" asked the teacher.

The students agreed.

"Scott learned a lot about belief systems, and I believe we learned from him as well."

"Thank you," they all said.

"Thank you for visiting us today, Scott. Remember, in whatever you experience, decipher true from Truth by separating your ego from the experience. Ask yourself "What does my intuition tell me is Truth, and what has my mind conceived that is only true?" Keep challenging yourself. Your intuition can be trusted only if you do not have an attachment to any particular outcome. Just be curious and inquisitive, desiring only Truth, nothing else."

Elyse stood up and walked toward my desk in the back of the room.

"Here is your next key," she said. "I've been saving this for you. It's a pair of blue jeans from your youth to remind you that you are still learning and growing."

"Thank you, Elyse." I turned to face the teacher. "I'd like to ask one more question, if that would be okay."

"Of course. Go ahead."

"Why can't I manifest things in my waking life as I can in my dreams?"

"You can. In fact, that is all you ever do. They are just more easily visible to you here. You think of this as a nonreal world. In here, you are not restricted by your limitations or your belief in the laws of nature. Think of what might happen if, in your waking life, you believed that you were unlimited."

"I can't even imagine that."

"When you can imagine it, you will create your own miracles. I know that your mind wants irrefutable proof and that having that proof will help you to quiet its questions. You've learned the concepts, but I understand that nothing replaces the value of personal experience. You can consciously choose which world you see, but you must believe it to be so to be able to truly see it."

The pigtailed girl then jumped in: "Believing is seeing!" she said.
6:59

When I woke up, I took out my journal and wrote line 3:

Uncovering the Truth

Portal 1—Aware is what we can be. Awareness is the way of Being.

Portal 2—Accepting is how we can act. Acceptance is the open
  arms of the Universe.

Portal 3—Belief is what we think we know to be true. Knowing is
  our Truth.

22

I got out of bed and prepared for an eventful day. I was looking forward to a meeting I had scheduled with Eric at the office later that afternoon. We had gotten quite close, and along with Karine and Nowell, I was happy to have some new and great friends. I thought briefly of Greg and how I wished he was on that list as well, but shelved that thought for another time.

After showering, I decided to search my closet for something unique to wear, something different and more exciting than my usual wardrobe. That's when I saw them. Obscured behind dozens of similar-looking khaki slacks hung what appeared to be the same pair of blue jeans I'd received in the dream. Stunned, I took them out and inspected them. They were faded and soft, and the Levi Strauss & Co. tag confirmed they were my size.

As much as I would have loved to believe that the jeans were manifested from my dreams, I did remember owning a pair a long time ago and wondered if they had always been there and I had just forgotten about them. This led me to a mind-bending riddle . . . did I know those jeans were there and so thought them up in the dream, or did I think them up in the dream, which created them . . . out of thin air? This was a question for Larry to weigh in on.

I was sure he would be at the school or on his way, so instead of intruding with a call, I sent a text: "I had an amazing couple of dreams, and I think you were in them. Something else happened, though. Really weird. I could use my best friend's insights. Let me know when you can speak."

Almost immediately, the phone rang. "Hey, I'd love to hear what you have to share, but it really isn't a good time for that. We got some really bad news this morning. If you are up for it, I think I could use *my* best friend."

"I'm sorry. What happened? Is everything okay?"

"I can't right talk now. Can you come by tonight?"

"Of course, I'll see you later."

As we hung up, I wondered what could have happened. Larry rarely, if ever, asked for help. The first thought that came to mind was that he and Ginette were having some issues. I considered that for a few minutes but then decided not to speculate or worry. Regardless of what it was, I knew I would help and support him in whatever way I could. Until then, I figured that the best thing for me to do was to fully engage in, and focus on, what I was currently doing.

I decided to create my own casual dress day. I put on the blue jeans, my Springsteen tee shirt, and a pair of my running shoes, then headed to the office.

I was the first one there. When I sat in my chair, I looked at the clock to see how early I actually was. It read 11:10. That struck me as very weird; perhaps it was the weekend, and I had completely lost track of time. Just as I was again about to consider my level of sanity, Karine sat down at her desk.

"Business as usual," I thought, although these days, nothing seemed usual. The office soon filled with a few others, and I figured my wall clock had just stopped. I made a note to ask Nowell to check the battery.

I stared at the numbers on the clock and was a little startled by Karine, who was suddenly standing next to my desk. She was dressed in a buttoned-down white shirt, slim black skirt, and a red blazer.

"Clock stopped, huh?" she said, following my gaze.

When that fact sunk in, I was stunned at the implications. In the dreams, my watch let me know if I was dreaming. Was I dreaming now? I thought back to the lucid dreaming workshop and tried to lift my desk with one finger. It didn't move. I then tried to levitate. Nope. I finally accepted that the clock was indeed not working and that I was truly awake. It was fortunate that I didn't try to fly out the window as a test.

"What exactly are you doing, and maybe more concerning, *what* . . . are you wearing?"

"Oh, I'm just having some fun, Karine. You should try it some time. And speaking of clothing, I want to commend you on your new style."

"Yes, it's called the 'no kidding look.' You really like it?"

"I do. Hey, how about you join Eric and me for our meeting today?"

"I'd love to, but unless you really need me, I have a lunch meeting with Nowell." Suddenly, the picture was clear.

"Hmm. Meeting, you say. Let me ask you this—is Nowell a person who might admire someone wearing a . . . let me see . . . a 'no kidding look'?"

That was the first time I'd see Karine blush. It matched her red blazer.

"Mr. Billings," she mused. "Seriously, it took you this long? I thought you were sharper than that."

"Just a little slow sometimes, my friend. Well, I'm very happy for you. He is one of the most impressive people I've ever met."

"That's funny, he said almost those exact words about you."

That was a telling moment for me, as I took in the compliment without judging myself as unworthy of it.

"Well, maybe we can one and a half date sometime," I joked.

"You'll find someone soon. I have a good feeling about it."

* * *

It hadn't taken long for word to get out about Concord's new representation, and referrals and inquiries had increased dramatically. Damon had plans to hire two new salespeople and a couple of new administrative assistants. Even though he hadn't said it, I knew Damon felt a deep sense of gratitude for what I had set in motion. He was visibly more relaxed, and on multiple occasions I even heard him kidding around with a few of the other people around the office.

Damon had left a note on my desk to see him, and when I entered the hallway, I could hear laughter coming from Damon's office. It sounded like Damon's laugh, which was a pleasure to hear.

I entered his office and saw, to my surprise, that he was talking with Nowell. Seeing that made my day.

"Hey guys! What's so funny?" I asked them.

"Hey, Scottie," said Damon, "Nowell and I were just brainstorming some ideas about how you should go about spending this."

I knew what was in the envelope he handed me. Though it would have been perfectly fine with me that Nowell knew as well, I was absolutely sure Damon would never have given him the exact details.

"Okay, I'll play. What did you two geniuses come up with?" I asked.

Damon answered first. "I said you should invest in some of the essential things, like a personality, a sense of humor, and maybe a mail-order bride. However, now that I'm looking at you, you probably could use an entirely new wardrobe as well."

"That's funny. Uh, guess what? I apologize for calling you a genius, Damon. And by the way, when's the last time you had a real date?"

I didn't think I'd ever seen Damon laugh that heartily. As he was enjoying himself, I realized he could have asked me the same question and it wouldn't have been a joke.

"Your turn, Nowell," said Damon. "Scottie, wait . . . you're gonna just love this one."

Nowell wasn't smiling when he shared his idea. "Well, Mr. Billings, I was thinking that maybe you might perhaps invest in a restaurant."

Damon laughed again. "See what I mean! You can't even follow a recipe to boil water!" I enjoyed watching him have some fun. Then I turned to Nowell and slapped my hand with the envelope, thinking.

"Nowell . . . you truly are a genius."

* * *

Eric, dressed in a slim-fitting blue twill suit, arrived late in the afternoon.

"So, how's the life of a dreamer?" he asked.

"Eye-opening," I said.

We talked for a while about our progress, went over a couple of new potential projects, and discussed a few of the things his movie associate, Rose, might want to invest in. He then let me know that he and his partners were more than impressed by the firm and that he believed I made the right decision to stay. He also said that I could add Damon or anyone else I trusted to the team to help manage the growing portfolio. I was sure Damon would be happy to hear that but had a feeling that he wouldn't feel the need to get involved.

"How about dinner at Las Puertas?" he asked.

"I think I'll take a rain check on that one, Eric. I need to get over to my friend Larry's house as soon as we're finished here."

"Next time, then. Hey, ever been to a movie premiere?"

"Can't say that I have, Eric. Sounds like fun."

"It would be fun for you, but it's work for me. I have to pretend to be important and then answer about a million questions. It's in early May. Want to go?"

"I'd be honored, Eric."

"Great! I'll send you a ticket, unless you need two?"

"Is everyone I know on the girlfriend bandwagon today?" I joked. "Only one ticket this time, buddy."

"Anything else to cover before I get going?"

"Actually, yes. How about you telling me everything you know about the restaurant business?"

23

The rain was coming down hard as I walked to the subway. A part of me really wanted to "jump the drops," but I decided on using an umbrella, instead.

Subway rides were much more interesting than they'd previously been, as I had made it a point to speak to at least one person per trip. I'd just turn to someone and say, "So what difference in the world do you want to make today?" Sometimes that person would walk away from me, other times they would ignore me, yet other times they would give me a dirty look or curse at me and then walk away or ignore me. But then there were the times when someone would have a really great, engaging conversation with me. One man even thanked me upon leaving the train, saying that I'd made his day and that he was going to ask that question of someone on every subway ride he took.

After hearing my question as I traveled to Larry's that night, a hunched-over woman with a few long white hairs on her chin answered it by saying, "I existed," and was silent after that. For a brief second, I could feel the essence of the beggar within her and though she got off at the next station, I contemplated her remark for the rest of the ride, wondering if "just" existing could make a positive difference in the world. I thought back to the woman at the cabin who shared her wisdom by just being and came to the conclusion that since we are all connected—all One—then our thoughts and feelings, our Essence, would be felt by everyone else, always. So making a real difference was at least as much about resonating with awe-inspiring power and love, or being, as it was about actually taking action or doing.

It had stopped raining by the time I got off the train. I navigated the few blocks to Larry's, rang the doorbell, and waited. Ginette let me in and motioned to the living room, where Larry was slumped on the couch. The TV was on, but he didn't look like he was watching.

"I'm really sorry I couldn't get here earlier. I had a meeting with Eric and couldn't reschedule it on such short notice."

"It's okay, Scott." He took a drink of a beer. "I didn't want to tell you over the phone because I was in the faculty lounge and there were a lot of people around. Paula got into Stonebridge but did not get the scholarship."

"At least she got accepted, right?" As soon as the words came out of my mouth, I knew they weren't going to be well received. I made a note to myself that I'd be better off saying what feels right instead of what I think is the right thing to say.

"Well, what good is that if she can't attend? Honestly, it would be easier if she didn't get accepted," he said with a great deal of sadness. "She was so close, Scott." He took another sip of his beer.

"I'm not sure what to say, Larry. Where is she? Should I go talk with her?"

"She's in her room, and I'm sure she'd prefer to be alone," he said.

I took a breath and sat silent for a while, waiting for the right words to come to me.

"Larry, I am really sorry. I know everyone is disappointed and that it's impossible for you to pay for that tuition out of your own pocket. I would like to share something with you that I think might help. Just a belief I have, but only if you really want to hear it."

"Sure," Larry replied, "why not?"

"I'm happy to be alive. Happy to have you all as part of my family. I know that regardless of how important or disturbing things seem to be, we are all here together, on different journeys perhaps, but on connected paths that lead to the same place. I'm not asking you to believe the same or do anything for that matter, but for me, I will work on no longer trying to figure out what I'm supposed to be doing or trying to force what I desire to happen. Why would I think I know what's best for anyone, including me? I think it's time for me to embrace all experiences, stop judging everything, and just observe and experience the awe and power of life."

As I looked at Larry, a small smile began to form on one side of his mouth. I sensed that he felt lighter, less worried. Ginette, who had apparently heard the entire conversation, came over, sat on his lap, and kissed him on his lips. "You know something, honey? Your friend is very smart. We all made it this far, and nothing will stop us from being a family."

She got up and kissed me on my cheek. "Thank you, Scott. Thank you."

I pulled out the envelope from my pocket, opened it, and took out the check. I didn't look at it but held it up for the two of them to see.

"Listen guys . . . nothing would make me happier than to loan you the money to pay for the tuition. I don't even care when you pay me back. In fact, Paula can begin to when she lands a spot with the New York Philharmonic. Please let me do this for you. You guys and Paula are my family."

Neither of them said a word, until Larry finally asked me to give them a few minutes. I walked into the kitchen and waited. Finally, they came into the kitchen, holding hands as they approached me.

"Scott, this is by far the most generous thing anyone has ever offered to do for us," he said.

"I don't even know what to say," said Ginette.

"Great," I said. "Can we go tell Paula?"

"I don't think that's a good idea," said Larry. "We are in one hundred percent agreement that we cannot take a loan from you."

"What? I don't understand. You saw the check. A loan for all four years as well as room, board, and other expenses would barely amount to a third of the whole thing."

"It's not the money," said Ginette. "We discussed it a long time ago and were in agreement back then that if she didn't get the scholarship, then it just wasn't meant to be, and even though it would hurt, we would accept God's will."

"I appreciate that, guys, but how do you know God didn't will me to give you a loan?"

"Believe me, I would love nothing more than to see my daughter happy," she said, "but you said it yourself a little while ago; why would we try to force something to happen? It doesn't seem natural to me. And what if she wasn't good enough for the scholarship and struggled against those more talented? Forcing something and then regretting it would be intolerable."

"And there's one more thing," said Larry. "I have seen friendships and families fall apart over money. What if I missed a payment? Or what if one of us gets laid off? Honestly, your friendship means the world to me, and I wouldn't want to jeopardize it because of money."

"I'm really not concerned about any of that. It would be my honor to do this."

"I'm sure that's true, but because I honor our friendship, I need you to make me a promise that you will never offer me money again."

24

It had proven to be an even more eventful day than I'd anticipated. As I got in bed, I was still thinking about Paula as well as the rest of the day's events. I fell asleep quickly, though.

Donning the mysterious blue jeans, I entered the fourth portal, where I saw nothing but green grass, trees, and rolling hills everywhere. It was a beautiful day with only a few lone white clouds in the sky. One of them looked like the torso of a woman. That made me smile, thinking of Lucena.

I decided to walk around and just enjoy the experience. I picked some yellow daffodils as I made my way through a field of perhaps thousands of them. Then, on the other side of a brief uphill climb, I saw a building on top of a much higher hill. It looked as if it came right out of a storybook. I thought about snapping my fingers or flying there but then remembered the conversation with the teacher about enjoying the ride, as well as the conversation I had with Larry and Ginette about forcing things. And so, instead of taking a short cut, I figured I'd experience the path before me.

I found the climb to be quite exhausting. At one point, I stumbled and fell to my right knee, tearing a hole in my jeans. Though it felt like hours had passed, when I looked up to check my progress, I wasn't even close. I again considered a faster approach, but the thought of "cheating" just made me even more desirous to reach my goal through a more patient process, without shortcuts.

As I finally reached the top of the hill, I lay flat on my back to rest. The soft white clouds were much closer to me, and I could feel and even smell their mist-like quality.

When my strength returned, I stood and faced the building. It was made of plain white cinder blocks, with a high row of windows all around it and a seemingly endless walkway leading to the door. Perhaps I was losing my touch, as this dream seemed less creative than the others, perhaps even a little bit clichéd.

I made my way to the front door. On it was a sign that read, "The Mind Game." The door opened by itself. More clichés. I entertained myself with the expectation of seeing an old man with a cape and hunched back offer a greeting like "Welllllllcome," but no one was in the empty hallway that loomed before me. I walked through it and saw a doorway at the far end. When I opened that door, the trite nature of the dream faded away. In front of me was an extraordinary room filled with two ornate red velvet couches on a large raised platform, with life-sized mannequins on either side. Art work depicting beautiful landscapes as well as several portraits of men and women lined the walls. Surrounding the platform was a viewing gallery of what appeared to be hundreds of audience participants, all apparently waiting for me.

And that wasn't the weirdest thing. There were two men standing on the platform, both dressed in sports jackets. They were identical. I don't mean that they looked exactly the same, I mean they were identical; just mirror images of each other. A strange melody began to play, and the two of them did a synchronized dance.

A woman dressed in a red velvet outfit that matched the couches walked to me, hooked my arm with hers, and escorted me in the direction of the stage. When I moved closer to the twins, the music and dancing faded, and they turned toward me, one holding a microphone in his right hand and the other holding one in his left. He was, I mean they were, the beggar.

"Welllllcome!" they exclaimed enthusiastically and then laughed in unison. "Just playing with you. But I'm very happy to see you here," they said at the same time. "We really have a great show today, and we're glad you could join us."

"I'm? We're?" I questioned. "Are you some sort of twins, or are you one person?"

They both answered: "Yes," beaming at one another.

I ignored the confusing response. "We seem to be in the middle of nowhere, and although the building outside looks normal enough, in here, well, this wasn't what I expected. What is this place?"

"The better question is *when* is this place? The answer to that is, of course," they turned to face each other before continuing to speak in unison and along with the audience, "*now!*" The twins continued. "We're now. Always been here, waiting for you, and yet we, and you, have always been here, now."

The two guys continued to move as a mirror image, which was wild. I got a bit sassy. "Let me rephrase my question then . . . Where the *now* am I?" I heard what I thought was some faint clicking after I spoke, but could not determine its source.

"You're in the Portal of Presence. That is, Presence in the moment, this moment, the only moment there is."

"Presence?" I asked. "You mean I am present, here and now?"

"We'll get to that. In the meantime, enjoy yourself . . . here and . . ." they looked at each other again when they spoke "*now!*"

The applause sign lit up and everyone clapped wildly.

"What are those?" I pointed to three golden curtains that had suddenly appeared, dangling in the air above the platform.

"Ah, yes. Those are the 'life review and edit' curtains. You see, every time you reach a certain point total, you win the opportunity to open one of those curtains. Each will take you to a memory. You can then choose to keep your memory or trade it in for a new one, thereby changing your past." The audience applauded again.

"Wait. . . . What?"

"We need a little help. Please explain further, Don Pardo."

A deep announcer-like voice sounded, but I couldn't tell from where it originated.

"Well," said the voice, "memories are aspects of the mind, stored in the brain. The actual event that you experienced doesn't exist; only your memory persists. You have the ability to 'rethink' a particular memory to be the way you'd like to remember it. When you do that, you actually change the brain to store the revised version of the memory. When you reinforce that by continually focusing on the new version, that version becomes your reality. So, for all intents and purposes, you will have changed the past. In fact, who's to say whether the past even exists, right boys?"

"Right, Don Pardo!" they said. "Changing your memory of an event shouldn't be too surprising to you. We all do it almost every time we think of a past situation, by adding in a different interpretation. Rare would be the case where you asked anyone about an event in their perceived past and they would give you an accurate answer."

"Do you mean that in this present moment I can change my experience of anything that happened to me in the past?"

"If you believe you can and retrain your brain, yes. Remember, it's your brain. Just a tool for you to perceive the world. Since the past does not actually exist, what you think right now is your only reality. You have control over the now."

Besides the lessons available to me in this portal, I now had an even more personal interest in this game, but I began feeling a little dizzy.

"Any other questions before we begin?' The right-handed twin turned to his left-handed partner. "Did you say before we *begin*? The audience burst into laughter. The other twin spoke, "I don't think I said that, as that would mean there would be an ending, which is . . ." Everyone there spoke at once. "*Just. Plain. Ridiculous!*"

"I'm not even sure what to ask. I'm a little disoriented. I'm having trouble focusing."

"That's because you usually focus on what was or what will be. In this place, you can only be present, something you are not used to being. When you learn to live in the now, being truly present, you will eventually experience the essence of Presence—that which is always and only present. You may be confused *at* the moment, but know that there is only clarity *in* the moment."

"Wait, how could I be in the past or future if there is only now?"

They both smiled. "Good question. You have not fully appreciated or experienced the moment you are in. Due to your ingrained memories or desires about the future, you are always letting your mind create stories about what you are experiencing. And so you're here, but you're not really here," the audience joined in . . . "*now!*"

"I want to say that this game is getting clearer, but there's a difference between wanting to say it and actually saying it," I said, playfully.

"I think we can give him some points for that. What do you think, folks?"

"Yeah . . . yeah," they screamed. I heard muted clicks again.

"You see, your mind dwells in the past and explores the future, but neither actually exist. Your mind does both of those things only in the present moment. You just aren't aware of the present moment and so are caught in an endless dizzying loop that is based on time and space, one of the greatest illusions of your mind. Let me ask you, how long did it take for you to climb the hill and to walk to the doorway?"

"Seemed like hours."

I could now clearly detect some sort of counter that clicked multiple times whenever I spoke.

"Because you perceive, and so believe, in time and space, you, in this case, literally created it in your dream. Look at your watch."

"It's not working. What does that mean?"

"It means you picked a dream symbol of great significance. There is no time in this world. That is why your watch doesn't work."

"So, there are indeed other worlds?" I asked.

"Oooh, lost a point on that one. Of course, you know the answer to that, but in case you forgot, no, there are no other worlds. In fact, there isn't even this one. Time does not exist anywhere. Tell me, why do you think the concept of time was invented?"

For the first time in a while, I heard myself speaking but didn't think it was me who was talking.

"Time measures what appears to be a linear existence," I said. "In the spatial-temporal illusion, people, places, and things are 'out there' and so take time to get to. People age. Memories are things that happened in the past. Visions are things that might happen in the future. But, in reality, it's all mind games."

The point machine was rolling with clicks and now ringing with bells.

I continued. "In a mind that sees, and so believes in, a past and a future, time is the tool that connects the dots," I said. "But time is like a movie reel, which is made up of many different frames of a film. Organizing those frames and projecting them in the way that the mind can relate to them creates the illusion that there is a beginning, middle, and end. Things appear to happen sequentially, yet there is only one movie reel, and all its 'parts' are just aspects of the one reel. The film has no beginning, middle, or end; it is whole, right here, right . . ." I put my hand to my ear for the audience to pick up the cue.

"*Now!*" they said and then roared with applause and cheers.

"Well, now," said the one of the twins. "Perhaps I should give him my coat and the microphone?" The other responded: "Well, go ahead, give it to him." Then the first one spoke again. "Yes, why don't you? I like mine." I enjoyed the banter between them. "Time for your next challenge," they said. "Think carefully about when you were at the door. Where were you?"

I pointed toward the door. "I was over there?"

One of the two men held up a big red buzzer and pressed it. It made an awful sound. The audience booed. "No, you think you were there, but remember your experience when you were at the door. When you were standing at the door, were you really somewhere called *there*?"

"I'm still not sure what you mean."

"Let me ask you this," they said, "at this moment, where are you and when are you?"

"I am here, now," I said.

The machine whizzed, and horns blew. I was racking up points.

"And no matter where or when you are asked that question, what would your answer be?"

"Always the same," I said. "I am here, now. So yes, when I was standing at the door I was doing it in the here and now. And my memory of being at the door is still happening in the here and now. I get it."

"You have not had, and will never have, any experience where you are *not* here and now. The place called *there* doesn't exist. Your existence and experience is timeless."

"*There* exists only if I experience myself as separate from all that is around me," I said, surprising myself with the statement.

The twins nodded excitedly. "Scott, you're playing very well today. You've earned the double bonus points opportunity."

The audience exclaimed, "Ooooooooo!" excitedly waiting for the bonus question to be revealed.

"Answer this question, and you will have almost enough points to open a curtain. And now for your question," said the twins. "We're not saying this is true. but if there *were* only One Dreamer and you *were* living within that One Dream, how would that affect your view of the reality of time and space?"

Ironically, in a place without time, a huge digital clock appeared overhead.

"Hurry. You don't want to miss the chance to earn bonus points! You must answer in time, Scott, in time."

"I don't really understand the question," I said as the clock started a countdown and the audience yelled: "Ten, nine, eight . . ."

I stopped trying to think and instead just started to talk. "Based on time, space, or both, I was led to believe in an objective world—one in which people, places, and things exist as objects somewhere outside of me. Objectivity was my reality, and subjectivity, my internal experience of the outer world, was fantasy. It is the opposite that is the truth: that 'out there' is the objective illusion, and the inner, subjective world, is more closely related to reality.

"In my mind, and that of the One Dreamer, it would make sense to create time just to make sure we got where we needed to go in an agreed-upon manner. Distance would be a tool for the illusion that we could actually *go* anywhere, as if there is anywhere that we could even go to.

"When I awaken to Truth, I no longer experience time and space. I can find Truth within the moment, the real moment. That's when I'll remember my True Essence as the One who dreamed of a man called Scott."

"Now let's see what the judges have to say . . . Yes! Well done. Congratulations. You win the double points, and you have just a few more points to go! Here's the next question. Get this and you'll be able to open the first curtain."

They opened an envelope and read, "Wow, a reverse opportunity! You don't have to answer a question—you get to ask one—and if it's interesting enough to our voting audience, you'll win the curtain. What question will he choose, folks?"

People in the audience started yelling out questions.

"Who am I?"

"What is the purpose of life?"

"What happens when we die?"

"What is the true nature of reality?"

"What is the I in I Am?"

"How does a wave of energy collapse into form?"

"Can entangled particles really work a microphone?"

I looked at them cheering me on and then turned back to the twins. "I know what I'd like to ask." The audience fell silent.

"What is it, Scott? We all want to know."

"Is there more to my life than what it appears to be? I mean, what difference do I make? Is what I've been experiencing here really anything other than just a dream?"

"Oh noooo," moaned the twins. "You asked three questions, and you were only permitted one."

"He question-stacked," said one.

"Well said," replied the other. "Hold on . . . I'm getting something from the judges . . . great news. Because you're a good sport, they've decided that you can still open the curtain if you can answer a replacement question."

Another envelope appeared, and they opened it together. "This question has two parts. First, you understand the idea that Awareness, Acceptance, and Knowing are your True Essence, your very core, and that you need to quiet your mind to reconnect with that truth. The question is, besides the undeniable truth of I Am, that you know you exist, what is the *only* other thing you know and can be absolutely certain of?"

The answer came to me quickly, and I wasn't sure from where it came. "Yes, I exist, and therefore I experience. The experience could be real, or it could be an illusion. It could be in my waking life or in a dream. And even if what I experience or how I experience something changes, *that* I experience is certain. That is something we all know for sure. Experience, along with existence, are the only two certainties in life."

"Excellent! Now for part two of the question. What is the difference between having an experience and experience, itself?"

I put my knowledge of the other portals to the test. "When I'm having an experience—experiencing something—it means my mind is usually creating a story from what is happening in the moment. The story isn't about what is actually happening; it is derived from my past experiences, which interprets the current one though filtered eyes. My current experience could also be interpreted by what I want to happen in the future. In either case, I'm not present, as my experience is not about what is, it's about what I make out of what is.

"Experience itself is the nonjudgmental Observer, knowing itself in the moment. It is Absolute and all-encompassing, the totality of I Am."

I was really on a roll.

"Just as it is impossible to twist a screw into a piece of wood using a hammer, I know that I do not have the proper tools to see reality. So there is nothing at all that I could experience using my senses that will be the truth. I can begin to bridge the gap, however, if I can truly experience something without attaching any interpretation or judgment to it.

"For example, if I'm walking down the street and a passerby pushes me, I might get angry, believing that he wronged me, and so strike back. But that was not the actual experience; it was the mind-created interpretation and judgment of the experience. The more accurate description of what happened is that someone walked by and pushed me. That's it. Anything else is a story I made up. And I know even that perspective is limited by what I can comprehend with my level of consciousness.

"The key difference between experiencing and experience is now. In the moment, interpretation and judgment fade, and only reality exists. The deeper I am in the moment, the closer I am to Truth. Anything that takes me out of the moment shifts the actual experience into something that I am mentally experiencing. In that case, I see what's true for me, but no longer know the truth."

Everyone, including the twins, applauded as one of the golden curtains floated down in front of me.

"That's it! You've earned enough points to open one of the 'life review and edit' curtains." The audience cheered. "When the curtain opens, it will replay any time in your life. Just think about something that you might want to change in a big way, or even just slightly, and that memory will appear."

The curtain slowly opened. The first thing that came to mind was Karine, and how guilty I felt for taking advantage of her by not compensating her properly for the actual work she did. When the curtain was fully opened, I watched myself hand her the pearl bracelet I gave her years ago as a thank you for helping us land a big account. I watched as she smiled graciously and sincerely thanked me for the gift. The thing was, though, that she did a lot more than just help with the account. She basically worked the entire deal from beginning to end. Even though she loved the bracelet, I felt guilty every time I saw it.

The scene ended, and the curtain closed. "Okay, Scott. It's your choice. Keep the memory, or create a new one?"

"I'd like to change it."

"He wants to change it, folks!" They didn't need the applause sign for that ovation. "Get ready."

"Wait. What can I create?"

"Anything you can conceive and believe. Too much of a stretch, and you will not meet those two criteria. It's time to re-create . . ." They pointed to the audience. "*Now!*" they yelled.

I closed my eyes and pictured something that I thought would relieve the guilt. When I opened my eyes, the curtain parted, and I saw myself handing Karine a beautiful diamond bracelet, one that cost nearly five times what I had spent on the other. In the vision, I sported a large smile. Interestingly, her reaction didn't change at all. When the curtain closed again, I didn't feel any better.

"What happened?" I asked.

"Just because you change something for yourself, it doesn't always change anything for others. Perhaps consider what really matters to the other person before you assume your intention will be understood and appreciated. If you are not sure, you can always just ask them. But there is some good news."

"Oh yeah, what's that?"

"It seems that your change didn't alter your great relationship with Karine. It could have changed it dramatically, one way or the other. We forgot to mention to you that when you change one thing, nothing or everything might change."

"Well," I said, emphatically, "I think that would have been a very important thing to know!"

They ignored the comment. "Okay, folks, it's time for a commercial break from one of our sponsors. Take it away, Don Pardo."

"Oh boy," I said, as the twins sat on the velvet couches while the deep voice once again boomed from nowhere.

"Friends, if you're enjoying *Uncovering the Life of Your Dreams*, why not take a deeper dive and put it into practice in your everyday life? The *Uncovering the Life of Your Dreams* companion program is free for our lovely home audience. Go to www.OneIdeaAway.com/dream to find out more!"

I looked at the twins. "Did I just hear a commercial in the middle of my dream?"

6:59.

25

The twins must have rubbed off on me because the next morning I shared a corny joke with Karine, who responded with a look of confusion that I thought was hilarious. I laughed, and her confused look switched to one of exasperation, which I enjoyed even more.

"That was the worst joke I've heard, perhaps ever. You'd make a huge contribution to the world of comedy if you just stayed out of it," she said, holding up her arms to better articulate the word "huge."

I then took a jolt from what felt like a Taser, and my jovial mood quickly vanished because, with her arms raised, I could clearly see the sparkling diamonds on her wrist—she was wearing the diamond bracelet I'd swapped for the pearl one in the dream. I suppose I could have felt an overwhelming sense of power or awe, but what I felt was panic.

The blue jeans had been one potential clue, but since I could easily rationalize that they had been in the closet all along, I wasn't convinced. There was no way to rationalize this one, however. I was truly overwhelmed and could barely catch my breath. Everything I thought I knew about life and reality had just blurred into obscurity.

"Are you okay?" Karine asked. I still couldn't easily breathe, much less answer. "Are you joking around? This isn't at all funny." She stared into my eyes. "I'm going to call an ambulance."

She picked up the phone in my office and began talking to someone. I reached out and put my hand on hers to signal to her to hang up.

"I'm okay, Karine. I just lost my breath for a second."

"I think you should get checked out."

Little did she know that I had just had the biggest "check" of my life—a reality check that blew my mind. I took a few deep breaths, and as the fear subsided, what was left was the state of bliss that I'd felt in my first meeting with the beggar. The experience lasted only a moment this time, but it felt timeless.

"I'm fine. I really am. In fact, I'm more than fine now. Don't worry at all, Karine—about anything."

She took a hard look at me, and I guess I passed her test, as I heard her tell the person on the other end of the call that it was a false alarm.

"What was that all about? You really scared me."

"It was nothing. Just a small anxiety attack. Really nothing to worry about." I asked Karine to sit down. "Please don't read anything into what I'm about to ask, Karine, but when did you get that bracelet?"

She stood quickly. "I'm going to call for help again."

"Please just answer me. I just want to hear you tell me," I requested in a calm and controlled tone.

She studied me again before responding. "You gave it to me, of course."

"Yes, I know I did. I'm just wondering when I gave it to you. I don't quite remember."

She tilted her head and raised her eyes. "It was a few years ago. We signed on a big client, and you gave it to me for my help with that. I believe that you and Damon had some issues with that client later on and he fired us. But I still think about how generous you were to give it to me, and I smile every time I look at it. That's why I never take it off, by the way. It always makes me smile, and around here, that's worth a lot more than what this cost you. You do really remember all this, Scott? You're just playing some sort of mind game with me, right?"

26

As I lay in bed that night, I rehashed the day's events. I realized that a part of me had hoped Karine would tell me that she recently swapped the pearls for the diamonds herself. But I also knew that part of me was the part that kept me small, safe, and powerless. I wasn't sure if I'd ever really understand how she ended up with the dream bracelet, but there was another part of me that didn't care to know, and instead, remained amazed and yet, perfectly content with, and accepting of, the mysterious experience.

I drifted off to sleep, and apparently the twins had been waiting for me. "Okay, weeeee're back. Scott has been on a record-setting pace." The roar of applause from the audience filled the room. "In the last show, you asked a wonderful question: Is there more to my life than this? To get this round going with the first challenge, today's studio audience requested that you answer your own question. Do you accept this challenge?"

"Okay, I'm game," I said to the roar of the crowd.

"Good for you. And we will help you get started with your answer. In your question, what exactly do you mean by the word 'this'?"

"*This* . . . Yeah, I see where you're going." I paused to collect my thoughts: "For as long as I remember, I've asked if this was all there is. The word 'this' referred to my life as I knew it—unexciting, uninspiring, and unfulfilling. So the answer to that question is yes; it was all there was, as my life was what I understood it to be."

The point machine started clicking.

"And yet, I now know that life as I knew it did not exist other than in my mind's dream. But my new answer is still the same. Yes, this is all there is. However, now 'this' doesn't refer only to my perceptions of my life. It's everything. The totality of Consciousness. Yes, this *is* all there is, and it is perfect."

The twins high-fived me during the applause and affirmative shouts. "You've already scored a ton of points for this round. Let's keep going. "If 'this' includes everything, then that means your in-dividual, mind-created life as well. What is the purpose of *that* life?"

I remembered I'd learned something about the purpose of life in another portal, but instead of trying to recall that, I cleared my mind and intuited the answer in the moment. "All that I Am chooses to experience all that there is, now. Experience. That is the purpose of life. One Dreamer, experiencing numerous limited dreams, all to remember the unlimited nature of Truth. From a more relative perspective, the purpose of Scott's life, the life I'm living now, is to share my experiences with others."

"And how should you share your experiences?"

"There's nothing I 'need' to or 'should' do. That said, I can choose to share myself, including my gifts with others, not because I have to, but because I can. Through loving-kindness, almost anything

I share will make a difference in other's lives. I can choose to live a life of authenticity, of Truth, as I understand it. Doing so will help others, and me, to enjoy the ride."

"Your next question is one that we'll ask later. Wait! There is no later. Here it is, then."

The twins were certainly having a great time.

"Tell us about being present and Presence."

"I will," I said. "But before that I'd like to know something. If there is only One, then why do you keep referring to yourself as 'we'?"

"He counter-questioned us, folks!" The audience roared in approval.

"There is duality in the dream, but unity in the Dreamer," they said. "We are still in the dream, Scott. This is your world."

Before my eyes, the twins merged into one person and then split back into two again.

"And then you realize," they continued, "that you appear to be more than one, but that's just a mind game."

I thought back to my lessons of the previous portals before speaking. "Consciousness is One. It creates split personalities, so to speak, to experience its Essence in many unique ways. We are those separate personalities, having worldly experiences."

"Wonderful. Now back to the question: present and Presence."

"Got it. Present is a temporary state of being for me. The separate Scott is present, and then Scott is not present. Presence, on the other hand, is *the* state of Being. The permanent state of Consciousness. It is the connection and oneness of all things, all at once.

"I know that the path to Presence, for me, is to be as present as possible. I am learning how to let the mind go and awaken to reality. I am listening to my intuition without imposing any of my judgments or interpretations on it; without searching for proof to confirm what I already believe. I am letting go of the illusions of time and space, as well as the idea that there is any difference between my dream or waking world. As I do all this, 'true' fades into 'Truth,' and I will be home again, or more accurately, I will remember I am already home. I never left."

"Excellent, Scott. One point of clarification. You said that your path is to be as present as possible—how will you do that?"

"By breathing deeply into the moment. Feeling my body. Noticing what is around me with appreciation of what I see. Whenever I feel my mind interfering, I will narrow my focus to breathing, feeling, and observing."

The audience stood to applaud and shout.

"A question was just handed to me from an audience member. This is from Gwen. Where are you, Gwen?" A young woman stood, and everyone hooted. "Gwen's question for you is . . . Are you single?" The entire studio audience erupted into laughter.

"Well, my answer to that is . . . of course, we are all, only and ever, One."

"Brilliant!" they said. "And now for the question to unveil the second curtain. We've discussed the phrase 'I am here, now.' So, the question for the next curtain is, how can the phrase 'I am here, now' be refined to resonate even more closely with the truth?"

I felt stumped and went silent. The twins looked confidently at me, as if they knew I would produce an answer. I began to feel very peaceful and then felt the comfortable intuitive chill.

"Now only exists within the duality of past and future. Since those are illusions, technically, there can be no 'now.' Now is all there is, but because the word 'now' cannot be related to any objective opposite, it's a word without meaning. Without it, only 'I Am here' remains. But since I've said that, *here* without the opposite *there* makes the word 'here' irrelevant as well. I'll go on record and simply say that 'I Am here now' is redundant and remain only with 'I Am.'"

Wild applause enveloped the room. "Well, that certainly earned the second curtain."

The next curtain floated down in front of me and began to open. The memory of the school water fountain and Chris Flaggart popped into my head. I watched the entire incident from start to finish, ending with seeing me sitting at lunch with Larry.

"We're all waiting. Keep it, or create a new memory?"

"That was certainly a painful experience, but before I make my choice, please tell me if my changing the memory would actually change the past, or just my thoughts about it, and if the former, the implications of changing it for the others involved."

"Very well. First, it will certainly change what happened to you. In your reality, your new memory would be what happened. You would have to agree to make the change to see what effect it has on the others. What we can tell you is that Chris Flaggart's life was changed in that moment, and he contemplated it for decades. It haunted him, not so much because of what Larry did to him, but because he realized he could have caused you permanent harm. He eventually decided that he would help other children who were being bullied and went on to learn various ways to do that. Chris is not fulfilled, however, and your decision to change the memory and experience would not guarantee that his life would be improved. To be honest, the possibilities of what could happen to Chris are too many to contemplate. We just can't know for sure.

"Larry's future would, most likely, be very similar to the one he now enjoys. Without the incident, he would probably still become a history teacher, marry Ginette, and raise Paula. In fact, nothing for him might change, except the two of you would not have crossed paths that day and might not have become friends."

"Then it's no choice. I will keep the memory as it is." That response brought the house down.

"We are nearing the end of our game, and we must say that we have had such an amazing experience. How can we thank you?"

"I still don't have the key to the next portal. Can you help me attain that?"

They looked at each other before presenting another riddle. "You will find that key when you take a risk and make something that was old new again."

The twins turned to the audience and waved. "Well folks, that's our show for today. Let's all give Scott one more round of applause for a job well done." They waited for the clapping to subside. "Thanks to our producers and sponsors, as well as the great support team, and you, the audience. Let's look forward to another great show next time. In fact, it's already here and . . ." Everyone shouted "*Now!*" They high-fived each other again. "Any final thoughts?"

Just then a teleprompter appeared, displaying the words *Uncovering the Truth*. I read it out loud:

> "Portal 1—Aware is what we can be. Awareness is the way of Being.
> Portal 2—Accepting is how we can act. Acceptance is the open arms of the Universe.
> Portal 3—Belief is what we think we know to be true. Knowing is our Truth.
> Portal 4—Present is what we can experience in the moment. Presence is the authentic expression of the Oneness of experience."

"Good night, folks," they said, waving again.

"Wait, what about the third curtain?" I asked.

A serious look came over their faces, and they asked the camera crew to stop recording. They lowered the microphones and spoke quietly. "We're not sure you're ready for that one."

"I'd like to open it."

"Very well," they said. The last curtain appeared, and as it opened, I realized why the twins were hesitant. It was the scene in my house when I was about three years old, standing outside my parents' bedroom. My father was screaming at my mother. He then noticed me standing in the doorway and began to walk toward me.

6:59.

27

Weeks passed and that dream still haunted me. The twins were right; I wasn't ready to deal with the enormity of that childhood memory. But perhaps I was ready to deal with a less intense but nagging current issue. I left the office early after changing into the running clothes I kept in my bottom drawer and took a jog over to a local bike shop. After being wowed by the advances in bicycle technology since I'd last rode one as a child, I left the store with a brand new Trek and as cool of a helmet as I could find.

"It's like riding a bike" is a very true expression. Even though I was quite scared to ride a bike again, after only a few minutes on it, I was surprisingly comfortable and looking forward to what I had planned for the rest of the afternoon.

I hoped that Greg would be very impressed with the effort I made to meet him where he was at, in his world. Greg was very sharp, so I believed that once he saw my bike, he'd recognize my intention and forget about any of the challenges or differences between us.

As I peddled my way home, I realized that I'd never explained to Greg how my own insecurities and self-doubts prevented me from taking the initiative socially or engaging in deep conversations with others. Instead, I just let him make a bunch of assumptions about me, one of which was that I didn't care enough about being his friend. When I really thought about it, I had to admit to myself that I'd really never let anyone, not any girlfriends and not even Larry, get close enough to me to know the unconfident person I was.

I decided that things would be different. Very different. No holding back anymore. No longer letting fear be my guide. I'd be me, unconditionally.

We'd go for a ride, have a great chat, and rekindle the friendship we once had. Now seeing that I truly was capable of change, perhaps we would even take the friendship to a deeper level. Maybe I'd even surprise myself further and end up on that bike trip with him and his friends.

With that thought, I expected to feel good again, but I didn't. I began to feel worse. Pained, even. A tremendous fear arose within me, and I had no idea why. I pedaled as fast as I could.

No one expects to see an ambulance in front of their residence, but everyone knows what it represents. So when I rode up to my street and watched one pull away, followed by a police car, my heart sank.

It seemed as if the entire neighborhood was standing around a man who sat on the stairs that led to our building. He was someone I'd seen many times with Greg, though we had never been formally introduced. I didn't know any details, but I didn't need them. The man caught my eye and reached his arm out toward me. I leaned my bike against one of the trees lining the street and walked toward him. Like the Red Sea, the crowd parted to let me though. He lowered his head but kept his arm and hand outstretched for me to grasp.

When I took hold of it, I was, just like in a dream, clearly able to see a vision of Greg as a youth. He was perched on his knees in a park. He held a magnifying glass to his eye to look at something on the ground.

I saw him later, in college, looking through a microscope as his science teacher leaned over his shoulder to ask what he saw. Greg enthusiastically, and with great technical detail, discussed the beauty of an insect's wing, which seemed to impress the teacher.

Next, I saw him tossing his graduation cap into the air with one hand, while the other held a diploma that said doctor of philosophy in entomology. I shook my head, realizing that I had no idea that was his profession or that he even had an interest in insects.

I was even able to sense myself riding my bike alongside of him. It felt so amazingly real. Then out of the corner of my eye, I saw a driver running through a stop sign.

"I'm so sorry," I said to the grieving man.

"Thank you, Scott. I appreciate that. Greg was always very fond of you," he said, holding my hand a little tighter. I sat down next to him, and we shared a few moments of silence.

I'd wondered if he knew Greg hadn't really spoken to me in quite a while and if he knew how we had left things between us. He must have sensed what I was thinking, as he murmured, "He had only nice things to say about you." I could see and feel his sincerity through the tears in his eyes.

A part of me felt that there were no real "accidents" and that everything that happened was part of a beautiful process that we could not comprehend with our minds. Another part of me felt that Greg was alive within me and that only his body had vanished.

Yet another part of me felt a tremendous sense of loss and the accompanying pain. It was a heaviness that overcame my body and crushed my soul. At that moment, nothing I learned in the portals mattered. It was my turn to cry. "What's the point?" I asked under my breath. Regret was my teacher, and guilt was the lesson of the day. I never resolved things with Greg, and now never could.

The man reached into his pocket and pulled something out. "I'm not sure if you knew this, but Greg was a scientist. He was quite brilliant and the most interesting person I've ever met."

Amazingly, he handed me the magnifying glass that I had seen in my vision of Greg as a child. "I think Greg would have loved for you to have this."

When I took it, I felt comforted and savored a slight but very welcome taste of peace. I decided to use the memento as a reminder to share myself with everyone I met, with no playing small or holding back. I'd remember to be both fully present and fully me.

The man said goodbye as a car pulled up, most likely to take him to the hospital or the police station. After that, everyone dispersed. I sat alone, staring at the magnifying glass. It was Greg's old tool and now new to me. "Making what was old, new again." I knew without a doubt that it was the key to the last portal, but it was also a reminder of a deep and painful loss.

As darkness fell, for the first time I seriously considered whether I wanted to continue on to the fifth portal. On one hand, I would hopefully see Lucena again, as well as fulfill my journey and perhaps even find the truth. Those thoughts were countered by the idea that life could be taken from us at any moment, so perhaps there was no point in going on, as nothing really mattered.

I felt I needed to choose my direction, one way or the other. I looked up, closed my eyes, and visualized Greg. I imagined asking him what I should do. In my vision, he didn't respond with anything other than a smile. I opened my eyes and absentmindedly looked at the ground through the magnifying glass. Something unexpectedly passed under its lens; something I'd never seen before in the city. It was a small greenish salamander, nearly identical to the one I had seen in the first portal with the young boy. Astonished, I looked again to the sky and smiled. I was sure Greg could see me.

28

With the magnifying glass in my pocket, I looked into the fifth portal, watching as it grew much brighter than any of the other portals before it.

When I passed through it, I found myself in a place that I had never been before, nor could even have imagined, yet it felt very comfortable. There were lights and colors before me, and beyond them stretched an expanse of bright, white light, but I could not see anything at all besides that, not even my own body. I felt no sensations, either, nor did I hear any sounds. What I experienced was beyond the senses I was accustomed to using. The setting was very hard for me to comprehend, and I figured trying to do so might distract from the experience, so I let go of my thoughts, surrendered to the moment, and became still.

Suddenly I sensed the beggar's presence with me. I could not see or feel him, but I knew he was there. I tried to speak but found that words were not possible, and instead began a nonverbal conversation through intuitive connection.

"What is this place?"

"It is Freedom. It is home."

"Freedom? From what?"

"From mind-created limitations."

"Is this heaven?"

"You can call it what you choose, as it has no name other than what you call it."

"What are the lights and colors?"

"They are all aspects of you. Everything and everyone you experience is always an aspect of you."

"I don't understand."

"What do you know about the nature of white light?"

I recounted some memories from my earlier-life science studies. "When white light passes through a prism, it refracts into various aspects of itself, each part vibrating with a different frequency that is perceived as a separate color. But the effect is only a temporary illusion, in that once the prism is removed, all seemingly separate colors are again back to the whole. They were never actually anything other than pure white light. I do understand that, but I'm not sure what that has to do with me."

"Just as light refracts to experience itself in many colors, your True Essence refracts into everything you could possibly experience, all aspects of you, to experience yourself in every way imaginable. When you, as a seemingly limited, fragmented color of Consciousness, remember the truth and become 'enlightened,' you once again merge into your limitless Self, with the Knowing that you were never separated.

"Oneness. That is what we are right now. That's what we always are. But only when we fully awaken do we experience it. How able are you to now see the light?"

I suspected he meant it figuratively, but since I really didn't know the answer, I answered more literally. "I know it is all around me, but I feel more immersed within the colors than the white. Why is that?"

"Here in the Portal of Freedom you are not yet ready to know the purity of Truth. But you are closer to its Freedom than you've ever been."

"Please explain what you mean by Freedom."

"Freedom, as it is defined in a world based on duality, exists only with its opposite, which would be incarceration or limitation. Absolute Freedom, however, is the nature of Awareness, Acceptance, Knowing, and Presence. It is the unconfined, unopposed, unlimited expression of Consciousness. In order to experience Freedom, as is the case with all the other portal concepts, you first work on being free, that is, freeing yourself of the many fear-based illusions that blind you from Truth. When you are free from all that you are not, your True Self as Freedom is revealed."

"Even with all that I've experienced so far, why do I still have doubts about my true nature as being more than just a human being?"

"Remember, all your answers are within."

I took a slow deep breath and said, "Like a shadow intrinsically desiring but deeply fearing the experience of the light of dawn, the egoic, limited mind fears the revealing of its True Self, as it believes that its identity will die in the process. I know that the answer is to overcome my fears, yet I don't know how to do that."

"I will help you to uncover the truth from your fears. Let us continue with the concept of suffering and your thoughts around why so many people, including you, experience so much of it."

"I'm thinking back to my dream about the man in India. His message to me was that pain is inevitable but suffering is optional. Perhaps people suffer because they try to hold on to their self-created and limiting ideas."

"Please continue."

"People hold on to and protect things that they have learned and are familiar to them, including the people, places, things, and ideas that do not work for them, complete belief systems that work against them, and future desires and goals that keep them from experiencing the now. I think the thing that's becoming apparent to me is that everyone feels less than whole. We all feel incomplete. We attach ourselves to anything we possibly can that we think can ground us and give us some security and are very resistant to letting those things go. But the truth is that nothing outside of us can do that for us, and if we continue to search for wholeness outside of ourselves, we will, sooner or later, suffer."

"Yes, only when you are free from attachments, resistance, obsessions, addictions, and other mind-numbing distractions can you clearly see your True Self. When suffering is released, you experience Absolute Freedom. How can you begin to release your attachments?"

"Based on what I learned in the last portal, I conclude that being present releases attachments, as attachments are things that people hold on to from the past or look to in the future in the form of desires and outcomes. There are no attachments and so no distractions in the now. Be it a person, situation, desire, or just a belief, whenever I feel I'm attached to anything, I will look at what I believe that attachment does for me and realize that it is keeping me connected to ideas that limit me. With that knowledge, I can more easily let them go, surrender to the now, and be present."

"That sounded clear. It is now time to discuss another fear-based experience, one that is dear to your heart. It is your feeling of isolation, which is caused by separation. You have been suffering with that feeling for as long as you can remember. Know that the illusion of separation is within everyone and that the suffering people feel from it is caused by the dissonance between true and Truth."

I needed another clearing breath and waited until I felt some clarity. "Yes, people feel a conflict. It is a conflict between what their minds tell them, which is that they are separate, alone, and vulnerable, and their inner voice, which tells them that they are one with all, eternal and invulnerable. That conflict creates the feeling of isolation and loneliness, which is actually purposeful, in that it causes or pulls people to want to learn the truth. We all inherently know that the truth will indeed set us free."

"Why do you believe you have had such trouble connecting with others and maintaining fulfilling relationships?"

"I've felt I was broken. Aware of it or not, I've relied on others to make me better, to make me whole. Knowing tells me I am already whole and that the pull toward others is only a basic and innate desire to share that wholeness through connection. Most, if not all, of my relationships have been very limited. I know I'm capable of much more and would love to connect with people, not because of a need, but because of an opportunity to experience more of who I am and share that with them."

"What, then, is the purpose of relationships?"

"To know yourself in relation to the other person. Others are in your life to help you feel more connected. We don't need them for that purpose, but they do give us a taste of what true love feels like."

"You've touched upon one of life's most important questions. What is the nature of love?"

"I used to believe that love was the ultimate reality, that love was Truth. Now, even though I know it is the most powerful driving force on earth and a feeling that is closer to heaven as we might be able to understand, in a sense, it is just another human experience, as love does not reveal Truth. Truth is that which reveals all things, including love.

"That said, love is the uniting energy that moves us away from beliefs that keep us fearful and instead moves us into the oneness of Being. It is the connection between us all—between all the seemingly separate parts of our existence. Love is an opportunity to share our subjective experiences with others, to free ourselves from some of the causes of suffering.

"Fear is a prison that holds us back from releasing the love within us. Other people, especially those with whom we are romantically involved, help us 're-member,' to 're-connect' to Source. That's why love is such a driving force for all of us. I'm not saying that we aren't already connected, only that we could all use a little help to remember that connection.

"In fact, that's it . . . it's not even another person that we actually love; it's the love within ourselves that another person helps to bring out. So, in a sense, love is a powerful means, but not an end. We're actually not even interested in love, only connection, which is derived from the experience of love. Once we feel connection, true connection, we are never alone, never separate, and never afraid."

I felt a deep sadness, as if something had just been triggered within me. I sat patiently with that feeling without trying to change it, as I knew the feeling was a sign that I needed to pay attention to my body's experience.

"I'm thinking about Greg. I feel the grief of losing him and don't understand why such a kind and good person would have to die so young."

"Your suffering is not because of his dying. It is because you are forgetting the nature of life and death. What is the reality of both?"

I tried to focus but couldn't. I took several more deep breaths, but I still couldn't let go of the grief. "I'm trying, but I'm blocked."

"You are not blocked. You are blocking. Where is your conflict?"

"It's between what I know, intuitively, and what I feel, emotionally."

"You don't have to agree with what you intuit. Just share it with me."

"My intuition tells me that both life and death are other illusions of the mind. Death cannot exist, because it is based on the spatial-temporal mind illusion. If there is no beginning, there is no end. If there is nowhere but here, we never go anywhere. The dream may end, but the Dreamer always is."

"Why does that concept create such conflict for you?"

"Because as soon as I think about that, I think about how ridiculous it is to believe it. How can I? Greg died. He's no longer here. Isn't that the truth?"

"What part of your body is you?"

"I don't understand."

"If your leg was removed, would your essence be removed along with it?"

"No, of course not."

"What about your other leg, and both arms, and perhaps even your torso?"

"I suppose I would still exist."

"How likely is it that your True Essence as Awareness, Acceptance, Knowing, Presence, and Freedom are concepts that exist only within your skull, and that all of your experiences, even that of existence, are just self-constructed beliefs?"

"No, that doesn't even make logical sense."

"Then where is your True Essence?"

I felt a calmness and a sense of clarity with my answer and finally realized that when I have felt that I was talking but not the one speaking, that I was allowing my intuition to speak without my mind interfering.

"Greg's body died, but it never really existed as anything permanent. Nothing that doesn't last is Truth. Only his inner Self is permanent. His Essence, Consciousness, is not of body or mind. It is his body and mind that is of Consciousness.

"I am eternal. It is only when I let my mind go that I am truly alive. Surrendering to this understanding is the path to fearlessness and Freedom."

"You were asked a question early on in your journey. You know to which question I'm referring. It is time for you to answer it."

"Yes, how do I know that I'm not just a dream character within someone else's dream? I believe the answer to that question lies in the word *just*. Consciousness has a dream, and I am a character within that dream.

"However, I am not *just* a character, because the dream never actually ends. Nothing begins, nothing ends. I permanently exist both as Scott within the dream, and as Consciousness, observing the dream.

"Consciousness is fearless, as it is existence, itself. When I realize my True Nature, I will never again fear death, as I will remember that I exist as I Am, always and in all ways. Within that Awareness, I am the Knowing that is eternal."

"Let us discuss your fear of authentic self-expression, which, at its core, is the fear of judgment."

"I guess at some point I learned to doubt myself. I've been hiding all my life from judgment, preferring not to be seen. Even though I desire it, I'm not sure who I'd be if I weren't playing small. Maybe I should just accept who I am and not try to change myself."

"My question was asked of the other Scott."

Another deep breath was in order. "I am the authentic expression of Self, experiencing life. My self-judgments have no basis in reality. They are just things I've learned since I've forgotten my True Self.

"That is more like you."

"Yes, but I still feel there are two separate aspects of me. The first is the I Am that sees the image in the mirror, and the other is the image, itself."

"There is no battle or conflict within you. You already know that you are both the awakened I Am and the not-yet-awakened human being. Living authentically means accepting all you experience yourself to be in any given moment."

"But you just suggested that I shouldn't be my old, fearful self, didn't you?"

"I only said that I asked my question to the part of you that knows the truth. I did not say any part of you was better than any other. Just see your whole self in your parts, and you will eventually awaken to the truth that there are no separate parts."

"I don't want to wait until I awaken fully. I want to know the truth of Freedom, now."

"What stops you from that experience?"

"The voice within me that tells me I'm not good enough. It's a quiet voice, but I seem to hear it loudly. I'm afraid of it being right. I guess, all my life, I've just avoided people rather than put myself out there and face their judgments. I didn't want to hear them confirm my own judgments about myself. I've kept my inner circle very close. In fact, it's pretty much been only Larry, and I'm still concerned with his judging me."

"It is very normal to feel the fear of judgment. Everyone does. Everyone hears the same voice telling them that they are not good enough. Some are just better at blocking it out than others. Though we all have it in common, that voice is not born from Truth; it is learned during our early experiences in life.

"Understand something else first, though. People might like or dislike you because doing so reinforces their belief about who they are or could become. They may like or dislike you because of how what you think, feel, act, or believe compares to how they think, feel, act, or believe. Or they may like or dislike you just because of the way you look, which was a preference they learned before they met you. In any of those cases, their judgments of you, even the positive ones, really have nothing to do with you at all."

"The not-so-funny thing about all that is that I've tried all my life to be what others wanted me to be and it has never worked. Ironically, they never even knew the real me well enough to formulate their opinions about me. If anything, I presented a false image but couldn't sustain it, which led to more judgment and, more often than not, disappointment when I turned out not to be who I had led them to believe I was. I know this is all a mind game, but wow, it's a tiring one."

"It certainly can be tiring when you are always acting and then waiting for the audience to judge your performance."

"Yes, I see that. The real question is, who do I want to be that would most closely express my True Self?"

"I do believe you are ready to live into that expression, and I know you already know the answer to my question: What would people experience if you were authentically you?"

"They would experience, through me, Awareness, Acceptance, Knowing, Presence, and Freedom. I would share those gifts with the world without hesitation. If I woke up tomorrow and that was my reality, I would be living a truly authentic life."

"Why would that be an authentic life?"

"Because all those things are one with my True Essence, so my life would most accurately resemble who I truly am. I would be an effortless expression of Truth with no need for approval or validation from anyone."

"Impressive. I approve."

"Everyone's a comedian."

"What you have created is a beautiful picture. Once you have left all your fears behind, only that which is left will be authentically you. You will feel like 'You' for the first time that you can remember."

"I would love that experience. Please help me."

"When you are ready to face your deepest fear, you will strip away the remaining control of your mind, removing that which you are not and have never been. What is left will be pure; everything; the Absolute; Freedom."

I knew immediately what was left for me to face. "Why do I have to do this? I mean, I'm happy now. I really am."

"You are happy, but you are not yet happiness. When you clear your mind from the remaining fear-based blocks, true happiness will be revealed."

"I understand, but there must be other ways to release me from my burden."

"The only way to let go of something is to first grab hold of it. How ready are you to face and let go of what you are not?"

The confidence from all that I'd experienced was lessening. It was as if I could feel my body beginning to return and within it, a sense of heaviness. My surroundings seemed darker. I began to feel vulnerable and small.

"What are you deeply afraid of?"

Even though I had no doubt that the chronic lack of confidence I'd experienced all my life was caused by my unresolved past, I still felt a defensiveness rise within me. I couldn't admit what I was truly afraid of now, which was to have wasted this entire journey because of some old fear that I couldn't resolve. I just didn't want to face that possibility.

"Nothing. I'm not afraid."

Just then, I felt something behind me. Something dark and cold. Though I couldn't clearly see him, I knew, without a doubt, it was the man in the black baseball cap.

6:59.

29

Even though I still couldn't face my childhood fears, I did feel as if many layers of dead weight had already been removed from me. I reached over to the night table, grabbed my phone, and texted Larry to ask if we could meet that night so he could help me process that last dream. Larry called me immediately. "I'm running out the door but wanted to tell you I have to work late so I can't meet tonight. I'm starting the interview process for a new guidance counselor. The so-called perfect and very professionally dressed person we hired quit the other day—said she couldn't take the pressure of the job. I'll call you tomorrow."

After we hung up, I closed my eyes, breathed deeply, and relaxed. The breaths became slow and rhythmic, and I soon felt a deep calm and peace. In that state, I asked myself a question: *What am*

I really afraid of? I didn't try to figure out the answer; instead, I took another few deep breaths.

An image eventually appeared. I was with Lucena. We were making love but not *to* each other. We were using our bodies as a means to reunite ourselves as One. I felt so peaceful. When I opened my eyes, I was free of fear, but I knew it would return. That's when it hit me: I loved the feeling of peace. By avoiding pain, I protected peace. Maybe I believed that if I faced my deepest fears, I would get lost in a painful process from which I'd never recover to feel peace again.

But I knew there was no giving up now. I would face whatever I had to face in order to experience the truth. I envisioned myself getting past the pain and imagined my life as if I'd already accomplished that great feat. I sat for a while more, meditating on that new reality.

With that, I felt an amazing burst of energy. I jumped out of bed, showered, and quickly dressed. I looked into a mirror and asked a question of the man that I saw: "What difference in the world are you going to make today?" It was time to enjoy the ride—to ride "In-Joy."

* * *

I waited in one of the booths of a local bagel shop until Eric entered and sat across from me. "Thanks for getting over here and helping me, Eric. Really, I can't thank you enough."

"You don't have to thank me for that, or for anything, actually. I just want to help. You've helped me in more ways than you know, so, if anything, thank you."

For the next couple of hours, we got down to the activity at hand. We carefully reviewed the plan Eric had devised for me, which included not only a complete financial picture but also his personal involvement. It was much more than impressive; it was a real gift. I was overwhelmed with gratitude.

"One more question before you go," he asked. "What happened to having the security of a home of your own?"

"Security does not come from owning something around you. It comes from owning yourself," I said.

* * *

My next stop was the famous Stonebridge School of Music. I hoped to get the real story behind why Paula didn't get the scholarship, figuring that Larry's family would be comforted if they knew the truth about what had transpired.

After a long and very enlightening visit there, I made my way over to Las Puertas. Upon entering, I saw Ava in the corner packing a couple of boxes. I felt a deep sense of joy knowing that that she would soon unpack those same boxes. "Hello, *compañera*," I said.

She seemed a little surprised, perhaps because I'd never used the term with her before.

"Ava, we have a problem."

"We do?" she asked.

"Yes, we do. You see, I have to try to explain something to you that I barely understand myself."

I took out a long document, along with some blueprints, graphs, and spreadsheets, and started telling Ava the story of the new Las Puertas. I shared what I'd learned from Eric, including how to get the restaurant reviewed and highly rated, how to market it effectively, how to orchestrate a huge grand reopening, how to use the current space more efficiently, and eventually, when the time came, which I expected to be soon, how to expand Las Puertas to handle the forthcoming growth.

I talked about how influential celebrities could be, showed her the invitation list Eric had put together for the reopening event, and went over how we would get the newspapers and other media to cover it all.

I then explained to her the graphs and projected income, as well as the spreadsheet that listed how much would need to be invested to do everything that would need to be done to make the place a must-visit for anyone near the area. When I finished, she sat back in her chair and shook her head from side to side.

"Why did you put all this together?" she asked.

"Oh, I didn't. One friend of mine thought it was a good idea, and another helped me with the plan," I said, knowing perfectly well that I didn't answer her question.

"I . . . I don't understand. This is a lot of money," she said, looking at the six-figure total. "I cannot possibly afford that and will not qualify for a loan."

"I think I might have undertipped you over the years," I said, as I handed her a check for the exact amount that was listed on the spreadsheet. "Don't get too excited," I said. "This is not a gift, and it's not a loan. It's an investment. I want to be your *compañero* and own ten percent of the business, if that's okay with you, of course."

She screamed, "¡*Lennon*! ¡*Ven aquí*!" He rushed out, and they conversed in their native tongue for a while. As she spoke, Lennon kept switching his focus back and forth between her and me. They both looked at me in silence for a moment before tackling me and my chair to the ground with a team hug.

"I'll take that as a yes," I said, as I lifted my chair and myself back up to a seated position. "But there's one more caveat before we make it official." I handed them an agreement that Eric had one of his lawyers prepare. I made sure the lawyer represented Ava.

"I'd like to request that this table will have a reserved sign on it every day at lunchtime, for me. Deal?"

I thought perhaps the next tackle might have broken a bone or two, but I was alright. The looks on their faces were priceless. They were effusive in their thanks, still not really comprehending all that had just transpired. I requested she ask any questions about the contract before she signed it and suggested she keep it and study it for as long as she wanted. She signed it on the spot. I did as well.

"We have a lot of work to do over the next few weeks to get prepared. I've already contracted a team to make most of this happen and think you'll need to hire at least three more servers. I'd like you to be the manager and the hostess, Ava. No more waiting tables. What do you say?"

She nodded her head as my cell phone rang. It was Larry, and he sounded upset. "I need you to come over here," he commanded, and hung up before I could respond.

I went over a few final details with Ava, left the restaurant, and headed to the subway to meet with Larry. It was a quiet ride, in that surprisingly few people were in the train car. There was one person there who stood out, though. The man in the black baseball cap sat about ten seats away from me, head down.

I felt fear and I felt peace, two things I didn't think were even possible to experience at the same time. I stared at him while he just continued to look at the floor. I didn't feel the need to confront him, nor did I feel threatened. I wasn't sure if the fear I felt was coming from me or from him. When it was my turn to exit the train, I did so without looking back at him.

Larry and Ginette were waiting for me on their porch. "You broke your promise!" shouted Larry.

"I did not," I said. "I would never do that. You told me never to offer to loan you money again. I agreed to that. You didn't make me promise not to give it to Stonebridge. And by the way, *they* didn't give me a hard time about it." I winked.

"I thought about the concept of fate that we talked about, and it occurred to me that before giving in to that idea, we needed a few missing pieces of information. So when I was at Stonebridge, I asked to speak with someone in the admissions department. I had a great and honest conversation with a nice gentleman there who told me that although Paula was extremely talented, there simply wasn't enough scholarship money available to fund all the equally deserving students. My hunch was confirmed. Paula deserved to be at that school. I have to admit, I did enjoy it when I then said, 'Well, I think Paula will be attending next fall.' He certainly enjoyed it as well when I handed him the full payment for tuition, room, and board."

"And before you ask, it's not a loan. It's a gift. And in my world, that's what family members do for one another, so if you appreciate my friendship, I'll ask you to honor my request to accept it and never bring it up again."

Larry and Ginette looked at each other, neither showing any reaction, but the energy between them was something I could easily feel, and it told a complete story. Ginette then jumped forward and embraced me while Larry just smiled.

"Can we tell Paula now?' I asked and then looked at Larry. "Time to have her follow your footsteps, in a way, and make some history."

After a brief and loud celebration, I asked Paula if she would play some music for us. She grabbed her cello, and from its strings came one of the most beautiful renditions I'd ever heard of Bach's Cello Suite No. 1. When she finished, she held the last note and transitioned it into a fast-paced country hoedown piece. I didn't even know a cello could be played that way.

It was getting late and I wanted to let them continue the celebration alone. "I want you all to know something," I said. "As great as this feels to me, I need to be clear that I didn't do it for your thanks or even for your happiness. Honestly, as much as I love all of you, I didn't even do it for you. I just felt like Paula needed to share her gift with the world. Doing so will make a difference in a lot of people's lives."

I knew I'd sleep well, knowing that I *did* make a difference in the world that day.

Larry walked me to the door. "How could I ever repay you?"

"I actually have a great idea about how you could do just that."

* * *

It took almost three weeks for Larry to pull it all together. It was Thursday afternoon when I got the call that he was ready. I put the magnifying glass in my pocket and secured the helmet on my head. I never rode my bike without both of those items. I looked at my watch to confirm I had timed it right, but it wasn't working. That's when I realized something about those beautiful Rolexes, one of the ones I had always dreamed of wearing; you have to wind them. Sure, I used some of the bonus to purchase something that many people would consider to be frivolous, but I felt that having a beautiful timeless masterpiece was the perfect reminder of my adventure.

I pulled up to a small apartment building, locked up my bike, and walked into the lobby. I scrolled through the list of tenants until I found the name I was looking for. I rang the doorbell, hoping for it to be answered, and lucked out when a few moments later, Chris Flaggart came to the door.

"How much do you love your job?" I asked, without preamble.

"Huh?"

"I said, how much do you love your job selling insurance?"

He stared at me for a while until a sign of recognition registered on his face.

"Scott? Are you Scott?"

"I am, Chris."

"What are you doing here?" he asked softly, stepping aside to let me in. We walked down a short hallway to a very nicely decorated, neat little apartment with a small waterfall statue. I loved those things.

"For the moment, I'm here so you can answer my question, please. On a one to ten scale, Chris, I would like you to tell me how much you love your job."

"Okay. Umm, I'd say four. The people there are great, and I like the company I work for, but I really don't think it's my calling."

"Yeah, that's what I thought. Okay, just be ready for the cab tomorrow morning. It should be here by 9:30."

"What cab?"

"The one that will take you to your interview at Larry's school to be the new counselor, of course."

"I already applied for that job before. They said . . ."

"Listen to me, Chris. I happen to know that you were an extremely qualified candidate when you interviewed for it the first time. Now, please just go for the interview again. I have a very good feeling about it. And here, I bought this for you." I handed him a conservative blue tie. "I think you'll find it to be a key to your success."

The last time I saw Chris, I was crying next to a water fountain. Now, he was tearing up a bit himself, next to a waterfall. A beautiful full circle, I figured.

30

A week later, I sat at my desk and looked at the clock. It still read 11:10. I remembered that I hadn't yet asked Nowell to fix it. I picked up the phone to ask Karine to remind me but then recalled that she had a doctor's appointment that morning and would be in a little late.

I got up to get a cup of coffee and saw Karine walking in. I watched as she approached her desk only to be cut off by a young man who sat down in her chair and began typing away on a keyboard. I heard her sternly expressing her dissatisfaction to the clueless man and figured I should intervene.

"What's going on?" I asked.

"I don't know. Seems this guy decided that he would like to work in my seat," she said, sternly. She then continued talking behind his back. "I asked him what he's doing here, and he didn't answer."

"Excuse me," I said, tapping him on the shoulder. "Please tell us why you're seated here."

He pulled out his two earbuds. "Oh, I'm sorry. Can I help you?"

"I'm Scott Billings, and my friend here asked why you are seated at her desk."

"Oh, hello, Mr. Billings. Nice to meet you." He looked confused. "Uh, I don't know. I thought I was supposed to sit here." He paused a moment and said, "Wait, are you Karine?" When she nodded, he told her that Damon said to give her the message that when she came in, she should go see him. With that, he put the earbuds back in and continued typing.

Karine turned to me. "What's going on here!?" she yelled.

"I don't know, Karine."

She bolted toward Damon's office, and I tried to keep up with her. "I hope he doesn't think he can just get rid of me now that you're a big shot on your own."

"Calm down," I pleaded. "I'm quite sure there's a good explanation for all of this."

She burst into his office and didn't wait even a second before confronting him. "What the hell is going on, Damon?"

"Yes, good morning to you too, Karine," he said.

"Damon, I swear. You'd better tell me what's going on."

I quietly stood with my back against the door.

"Well, what's going on is that we replaced you," he said.

"You what? You fired me because Scott is the hero now and you don't need me anymore? Are you kidding me?"

"Who said you were fired?" he asked. "I just said we replaced you—at your desk job. I think you already met Jeff. He's a nice kid. I think he'll work out well. He works for you now, and for Scott too, of course."

Damon slid over a contract. Karine began reading it. As she made her way through the first page I saw her wipe away a tear. "Damon, is this for real?"

Damon just leaned back in his chair and put his arms behind his head, proudly.

"I'm so sorry about what I said. I . . ."

"Forget it, Karine," he said. "Just enjoy your new role, partner."

She began to move around his desk, arms outstretched to hug him, but he stopped her.

"I'm a hundred percent for this, Karine, but don't thank me." He pointed to me. "That guy did it."

She turned and barreled toward me. I learned my lesson from Ava and Lennon and braced myself to avoid another takedown. She put her arms around me and softly sobbed on my shoulder. When she let go, I handed her an envelope.

"I believe this belongs to you." Within the envelope was a check in the amount of the remainder of my bonus. Even after Paula's tuition for a full four years, the Las Puertas investment, and my watch, there was still more than a third left for her. She stared at it, mouth open.

"Scott, what is this?"

"You've earned it over the years."

As she stared at the check, I saw the reality of the situation begin to sink in.

"No. This is beyond ridiculous. I can't accept this."

"Consider it a signing bonus."

"Are you losing your mind?" she asked.

"I hope so," I replied.

Damon picked up the phone. "Jeff, would you mind coming in, please, and escorting Karine to her new office?"

And that's when the tears really overwhelmed her. Damon handed her a box of Kleenex, which she gratefully accepted as she and I left his office. I walked with her and Jeff to her new office, thinking she'd want to sit down and chat, but the first thing she did was to go over to the window and look out at the city. She looked so comfortable that I decided to let her enjoy her time and instead headed back to Damon's office.

"That was an amazing thing you did, Scott," he said.

"Yeah, that was fun," I replied.

"Want to grab a bite to eat? he asked. "Guess I'll need to pay."

My old friend was truly back. Over the last several months, his entire energy had shifted. This was the guy I knew in college. Seeing him this way led me to decide to do something I had been considering for a while.

"Hmm. You know what? I think grabbing a bite to eat is going to turn out to be a very interesting idea," I said.

"What do you mean?" he asked.

"You'll see. Gimme a minute. Just gotta make a quick phone call."

I returned to Damon's office to find him with his sports coat on, ready to leave. "Las Puertas has a huge grand reopening tomorrow. There will be about a dozen A-list celebrities there and a ton of press. The lines are expected to be a half a block long. But the people who own it said they'd let us in for a preview lunch today. We'll be the only ones there."

When we arrived, it was Lennon who greeted us at the door. "My mom and her team are in the back. They're just going over the plan again for tomorrow, but she said she'll be out in a few."

He sat us, bear-hugged my head, and went back to the kitchen.

"What was that all about?" asked Damon.

"Nothing much, *compañero*," I responded.

"What?"

"Forget it," I said. "I have a question for you. So now that we've made you even richer, it seems you're a lot happier. How true is that?"

"Well, I'm not allergic to money. But the truth is that it doesn't seem to matter as much as it used to." He took a few moments before continuing. "I can't really explain it, but I feel like something has been lifted from me since you got the Concord deal. It's not about the money. Not at all. Landing a deal like that raised the entire reputation of the firm, as you know. I keep thinking my father would finally be proud of me. I guess that was more important to me than I realized."

"That's a great insight, Damon. And what do you think now about making him proud?"

"It's bullshit," he said, nonchalantly. "Really. I just don't know why it even mattered, why I thought I was worthless without his approval."

His words sent shivers throughout my body. I hadn't thought about it before, but when he said what he did, I immediately related to it and wondered if it was the cause of my deep-rooted self-doubts.

"Scott, it's not the time to get too deep here. We're celebrating."

"We are? What about?"

"We're just two old friends, celebrating each other. No other reason needed," he said.

He was more than back. I had never experienced him like this before. That, along with Karine's bracelet, the jeans in my closet, Nowell, the connection with Greg, feeling a part of the beggar within everyone, and probably everything else that was manifesting in my life made me realize that I was truly living the life of my dreams.

Lennon brought us some drinks and gave us copies of the new menus. They were beautiful. It was then that I really took the time to look around and see how the place had been transformed. The bright colors had been replaced with a sophisticated neutral palette. New glass-topped tables stood where the old wooden ones had been. The entire place looked modern and inviting. The redesign also allowed for a few more tables, but not enough to handle tomorrow's reopening, which, according to Eric, was a good thing.

"We had some great times, didn't we, Scott?"

"I remember a lot of them, Damon, as if they're happening right . . . *now*," I said, humoring myself. "What do you think ever happened to those days?" I asked, not really wanting to open up a quantum can of worms along with the new Las Puertas.

"Guess we had to grow up."

"How sure are you about that?" I asked as I reached out to shake his hand. After our famous Phi Five and the ensuing laughter, I decided to forward the action.

"Damon, what do you believe is the purpose of relationships?"

"I really don't know. To experience misery?" he joked.

"Seriously."

"I wish I knew. Haven't been in one since Beth and I divorced. Just haven't found the right person, I guess."

Ava came over to the table, ready to take our orders. She started to speak, then stopped as Damon's eyes met hers. I watched as they stared at each other. I stood, took Ava's order pad from her and asked her to sit. "May I take your order, please?" I asked. Lennon, head peeking around the corner, looked on in delight. He gave me a thumbs up. I winked back.

Without moving his gaze from Ava, Damon softly asked "Scott, what are you doing?"

"I'm sorry, sir. I don't like to intrude on the customers when they are about to engage in deep conversation."

One of the three new servers came out from the kitchen and took over my duties as I began to walk out the door. I didn't think Damon or Ava knew or cared that I was leaving.

31

That night, I went to bed smiling. I quickly fell asleep and found myself back within the fifth portal. It was different this time; I still wasn't sure where I was, but everything was clearer and I could see, hear, and speak.

"I'm ready," I said.

"Of this you are certain?" asked the beggar.

"I am."

The beggar then changed appearance in front of my eyes. His clothing turned gray, he held a book in his hand, and a black baseball cap materialized on his head. He slowly raised his head.

"I am your suffering. I was raised in fear and have been following you your entire life. I have been waiting for you to release me."

"What happens to you when I do that?" I asked.

"Like a lone wave in the ocean, I will once again recede into the beauty of the One."

"How do I let you go?"

He showed me the book he'd been carrying with him. Its title was *The Witness*. He told me that the book held my pain, as well as the secret to releasing it. He held it out for me. "Whenever you are ready." Without hesitation, I put my hand on it and closed my eyes.

I was at Eric's movie premiere. I sat near the middle, on the left side of the auditorium. The man in the black cap was not anywhere to be seen, but I could feel his presence within me. I wasn't sure if I was still dreaming or not and didn't even bother to check my watch, deciding that it just didn't matter.

Eric was on the stage, talking. "Well, that's all I have time for before we start the movie. I'll be around afterward for any further questions. I hope you enjoy watching this as much as I enjoyed making it."

The theater darkened and the light from the screen lit up the room. The movie title appeared in front of us: *The Witness*.

In a flash, I was in the movie. I couldn't see the audience, but I could feel them there, watching.

In the first scene, I was in my office with Lucena. She was looking out the window into the dark night, then turned and disrobed. She slowly approached me, and I saw Karine watching us.

The scene changed, and I was in my room at my old house. I was very young, perhaps around three years old. I heard yelling and walked cautiously toward my parents' bedroom. I was very scared and thought my father was hurting my mother.

Now it was me doing the watching. I stood outside their door, looking on in horror as they screamed at each other and my father went to grab my mother's arm. She pulled away, banging it on the side of the bed, then slid to the ground sobbing and curled into a ball. It was at that point that my father must have seen me out of the corner of his eye, because he turned from her to look at me in the doorway.

"What the hell are you looking at?" he yelled.

I finally understood the origin of that chilling line.

"Yeah, you!" He continued to yell. "It's *your* fault we fight. Who wanted you, anyway?" His look changed from one of anger toward my mother to an uncontrollable rage toward me. "It's not polite to spy!" he said intensely as he moved toward me, slowly pulling his belt from its loops.

He raised his arm and then swung. As the belt approached, I quickly grew bigger and taller than he was. I moved forward and caught his arm before the blow could connect. His eyes were wide open, and he shook in panic. I could feel the fear from within him.

"You will not like where this goes," I said. "You and mom will get divorced. She will find someone who is very angry and will control her for the rest of her life until she decides to end it by taking an overdose of medication. You will go from relationship to relationship, trying to find what is eating you alive, but you will never find it in another person. Instead, the monster inside you will grow and attack all your organs until your body gives out. On your deathbed, you will have found no peace, because you never looked within to find it."

My father sat down on the bed and helped my mother up to sit next to him. She put her head on his shoulder. He wiped the tears from her eyes with his shirt sleeve.

"The mind thrives on conflict," I said. "But you are not your minds. See what I see," I said. "You are more than you can possibly believe."

"What should we do?" my father finally asked, softly, as they both looked up.

"First, realize that your intention is not to hurt each other. You love each other very much. What you are doing is projecting anger onto the person closest to you. Many people do that. But know that it isn't your anger that drove you to this point; it is your fear. You are together but still feel isolated and separate, not only from each other but from everything and everyone else. You are afraid because you feel you are alone and vulnerable. Because of that fear, you believe your life to be random and meaningless, with no purpose. That is what you learned as children, and it has been haunting your dreams ever since. Have comfort in knowing that dreams are of your own creation and that you can awaken any time you like. When you do, you will feel the connection of love within you. You will feel the truth."

"What is the truth?" asked my mother.

"That there is not two of you."

They took a breath in unison. When that happened, I could feel the audience watching with bated breath.

My father embraced my mother. "I'm so sorry. It wasn't me. I love you." She put her arms around him and reached up with one hand to put it behind his head, comforting him like a little child.

The scene changed, and the three of us were on vacation. We were on a rowboat, fishing, laughing, and telling jokes. My father told us a scary story, the same one he always told when we were vacationing, about a one-handed lunatic who roamed the area murdering people. He then showed us his arm, his hand covered with his shirt sleeve. Mom and I shrieked and laughed at the same time.

We rowed our way back to the shore and then took a short walk to a nearby store that sold souvenirs, clothing, and camping equipment. Mom and Dad held hands in one area of the store, gazing at picture postcards of the campsite. After looking around, I went to the cashier to ask if they had any fisherman's hats like the one my dad was wearing. The young girl behind the counter asked me to wait while she asked in the back.

A little while later, the man in the black cap came out. "Hello, Scott. I hope you created a fond memory."

"I did, thank you," I said. "I was wondering if I could get a memento of this trip."

"A fisherman's hat," he said. "Yes, that would be perfect. I don't carry any, but hold on a second."

He took off his baseball cap and gave it to me. He snapped his fingers and it transformed to look just like my father's hat. I put it on and it fit perfectly. The man looked at me fondly.

"Remember, you can manifest the reality of your choosing."

"Will I ever see you again?" I asked.

"I will always be with you. We are never apart. When you look into the mirror, you will see the truth: I Am. We Are."

I was grade school age in the final movie scene. My dad picked me up in his truck, and I warily shared with him what happened that afternoon at the water fountain between me, Chris Flaggart, and Larry Phillips.

"All scared little boys," he said. "It's okay, son. You will all remember the truth soon enough. You will see." He then started the car, turned the radio to our favorite station, put his arm around me, and headed home.

The lights came on, and I wondered if I'd fallen asleep in my seat and if the whole movie was something I dreamed. Regardless, it was gone—all the fear, as if it was never there. I was absolutely free. The loud applause shook my seat, and I stood to applaud as well. Eric got up on stage and took a bow.

I looked on the floor and noticed the program I must have dropped when I stood for the ovation. I picked it up. It read . . .

Uncovering the Truth

Portal 1—Aware is what we can be. Awareness is the way of Being.

Portal 2—Accepting is how we can act. Acceptance is the open arms of the Universe.

Portal 3—Belief is what we think we know to be true. Knowing is our Truth.

Portal 4—Present is what we can experience in the moment. Presence is the authentic expression of the Oneness of experience.

Portal 5—Free is the release of all that you are not. The Absolute is Freedom.

* * *

When the long ovation subsided, Eric thanked everyone for being there and then asked for questions. Dozens of hands went up. While he conversed with the audience, I quickly scanned the room and noticed someone on the other side of the auditorium, in the same row and in the mirror image of the location I was seated in within that row. She was a mesmerizing Asian woman with short black hair. Her long diamond earrings sparkled from across the room with stones that resembled those from Karine's bracelet. I felt drawn to her and knew exactly who she was. I could no longer hear Eric talking.

She turned, saw me looking her way, and gave me a quizzical smile. Just as I began to walk toward her, Eric finished speaking and the large crowd began to move around. Many moved toward Eric, while most went in the other direction, toward the exits.

I observed her moving toward the stage, so I turned the other way to go down the left aisle, hoping to get to her more quickly. I tried to keep track of her in the crowd, but by the time I got close to the stage where Eric stood, I had lost sight of her.

"Hey, buddy," said Eric as he tapped me on the shoulder. "How did you enjoy the movie?"

"It . . . was great, Eric," I said, still looking around. I refocused on him. "I mean, it was absolutely amazing. I felt like I was in it. It was freeing."

"That's great. I was hoping people would relate to it." Eric put his arm around a woman who was standing nearby. "I'd like to make the formal introductions. Scott, please meet my dear friend, Rose."

"Hello, Scott," said the famous movie star. "Eric has told me so much about you. I'm really looking forward to the opportunity to work with you." She handed me her business card.

"Thank you," I said, looking at the card. "It would be my pleasure." I then started looking around the room again.

"I'm considering investing in a few apartment buildings. Eric and I were discussing it last night, and we hope you can find some time to help." She must have noticed my distraction. "Are you looking for someone?"

"Oh, I'm sorry. Yeah, I thought I saw someone I know." I again refocused. "Yes. I'll of course be happy to help you, Rose; it would be my honor. Eric has already filled me in on some of what you're looking for." Unlike with Karine and Nowell, I put two and two together a lot faster this time. "Wait, did you just say you were with Eric?" I turned to him. "I thought you mentioned to me that you were going out on a date last night?"

All three of us were silent and had similar smirks on our faces.

"Discretion is key in my business," I said. "Not to worry, but I am curious, how much could a story like this get me from the tabloids?"

They looked at each other and then at me. Eric winked.

"So, who were you looking for, Scott?" he asked.

"Well, there was a woman here, but I can't find her now."

"What does she look like?" asked Rose.

I had trouble answering, as I wasn't sure which version of the woman I wanted to describe.

"She looks . . . just beautiful," was all I could conjure up.

Eric let out a hearty laugh. "It's a movie premiere. That description really narrows it way down," he said, teasingly. "Thanks for the clue."

"I'm sorry. I don't know how else to describe her."

32

I was in my office, looking outside my window. The city was the same, but I wasn't. I could see many of the things I'd always seen, like people and cars, but I now saw birds, windows in the building across from mine, and even a couple of cats and dogs. Everything seemed alive, including the few small trees below that decorated the side of my building. Unlike before, I was no longer looking for a distraction. This time, I was enchanted with everything I observed. The experience itself was more than enough; I wanted and needed nothing else out of it.

I thought about Eric's movie and wondered if it had an even more dramatic effect on me than I imagined. With that thought I felt another pull, which was to make my way over to Karine's office. I didn't know why.

"Hey. What's up?" I asked.

"Oh, hi. Not much. Well, perhaps it is much. I've been thinking about how fortunate I've been and how I owe a lot of that to you. I feel so much better about things, and it's not only because of the money or the new role; it's mostly because I've now given myself permission to be me. I feel . . . freed. Do you know what I mean?"

"I believe I do. Karine, how do you know you're *not* dreaming?"

"What?"

"Nothing. Just thinking out loud." I walked over to her window and checked out her view. She followed me and looked outside as well.

"What do you see, Scott?"

"I see freedom, Karine. Everywhere. And I know that I can experience that any time I choose by letting go of any attachments, desires, goals, doubts, or fears. As I release all that I *think* I want or *think* I am, I uncover and reveal the freedom of that which I truly am."

Karine put her hand on my shoulder, and we stood there silently for a few moments.

As I continued to look at the clouds, I tilted my head and recognized a few that reminded me of those I'd seen in my dreams. I was about to say something about that but then noticed that one of the clouds began to grow bigger and stand out from the others. It became brighter than those around it and seemed to shape itself into the torso of a woman. I felt a comforting tingle run through me.

I turned to Karine and gave her a big hug. "I have to go," I said with a sense of urgency.

"What? What's the rush?"

"I need to go meet someone. A woman."

"Well it's about time! What's her name?"

I threw my hands up. "I'm not sure," I said as I left her office. I ran downstairs, hailed a cab, and jumped in. I told him to go to the Bethesda Fountain.

It was a beautiful spring day in Central Park. I sat by the fountain and waited. After an hour or so, I felt a little confused and surprised that I didn't see her. I wondered if I had misread the sign and just imagined what I saw in the cloud.

All thoughts stopped as I looked into the water. It sparkled with energy. I heard birds singing and looked around me. Children laughed and played, lovers walked arm-in-arm, and nature was alive, everywhere. Even the concrete I sat on seemed vibrant. In the moment, I saw and experienced it all.

I enjoyed the scene for a while longer and then walked to the street to catch a cab home. After a long wait, one pulled up, but as I started to get in, a woman grabbed the handle along with my hand.

"I'm sorry," she said, "I didn't see you."

It was the woman from Eric's movie premiere. I was too dumbfounded to reply.

"Look, I really would like to get home," she said. "It's been a good but long day. . . . Wait, . . . do I know you?"

In my daze, I shrugged my shoulders. She studied my face.

"Listen . . . which way are you going?" she asked.

I'd learned about seeing. I'd practiced acceptance. I'd begun re-creating my belief system. I'd watched twins dance to a mysterious melody. I'd contemplated amazing concepts and even crossed the gap between my waking and dream worlds. And with all my new-found experience and wisdom, the only thing that came out of my mouth was "Huh?"

"I was thinking we might share the cab. I'm going downtown," she said. "So which way are you going?"

"Uh, I live that way." I pointed in the opposite direction.

"Oh well, that's too bad," she said. I moved out of her way. She opened the door and entered. The cab began to pull away and I watched her watching me until she was out of range.

"What did I just do?" I said to a passerby on the street. He ignored me. I then reached down to my pocket and felt the magnifying glass. I didn't know what I'd just done, but suddenly I knew exactly what to do. I snapped my fingers.

"So which way are you going?" she asked.

"I know this might sound a bit crazy, but I'm going whichever way you're going."

She smiled beautifully, just as she did when we made love for the first time. Then she held out her hand.

"Hello, crazy man. I'm Skye."

Now: Scott Free

A man stands before an ocean, looking out, wondering about life.

A man stands before an ocean, looking out, in wonder about life.

I stood before the five iridescent portals. They blinked on and off like the stars I'd seen in space. I wore all of the mementos I'd received on my journey: Karine's polka-dotted tie to remind me that success begins with getting out of my comfort zone, the sandals the boy gave me so I could remember to tread lightly on my perceptions, the Springsteen tee shirt from Jean to keep me open-minded and accepting, and the blue jeans from Elyse to help me remember that I was still learning and growing. In my hand, I held Greg's magnifying glass to remember to share myself with no holding back. Finally, on my head was my treasured fisherman's hat, as a reminder that we can live the reality of our choosing.

I moved closer, and the portals began to shake. They hummed in unison with power. I could feel energy building. Portals one and five began moving slowly toward portals two and four, until they merged with them. Now there stood only three portals, still flashing, brighter than I'd ever seen them.

As if it was being absorbed, the middle portal began to fade as the other two grew in intensity, both in brightness and sound. These two portals seemed to encompass all facets of the other five, but they were unique unto themselves. They had a quality that was not at all dream-like, and I knew I was awakening from my lifelong dream.

The two newly merged portals then began to move toward each other. The ground shook as they did so, and I fell to my hands and knees. I looked up and saw that only one large, awe-inspiring portal remained. Its border was shining brighter than the big bang I'd witnessed before; its glow extended in all directions as far as I could see. The humming turned into a sound unlike any I'd ever heard. It was not quite a song, but it did sound musical. I thought I could detect the sounds of all seven notes of the scale; each note resonated separately but also all at once, together.

I stood there for a few curious, open, and optimistic moments, then moved toward the portal. The entryway of this one was different. Instead of looking like glass or liquid, this portal had a mirror-like quality to it that clearly reflected my image. Time to reflect.

The message came through me, and I heard my own voice coming from the portal. "By first asking if this was all there is, I was questioning my purpose and meaning in life. This was the beginning of my awakening. I sought to remove the pain of the human drama. That was also part of the journey. I then made a new quest, which was to replace that pain with peace, joy, love, and bliss, all of which were closer to my True Essence, but now I realize, still all limited as emotional experiences.

"As the nurse told me, we all want pleasure, and we all seek to remove pain. Awakening, however, has nothing to do with pain or pleasure, as both are still part of the dream. Although it might feel glorious to awaken, being awake isn't anything other than the remembrance of Truth. Not a hope and not a feeling, but a Knowing that I am more than the reflection in the mirror."

I looked at myself reflected in the portal, thinking that after the many answers I'd received, all I knew of the truth was that I existed and experienced. As I stood there, I wondered if there was anything more that I was ready to grasp. Just then a question reverberated from within the portal.

"Who am I, really?"

My reflection, along with the mirror, faded, revealing a clear entranceway. I walked through it and found myself standing in the exact spot where the entire adventure began. The beggar was right next to me. It felt as if we'd never left.

He held out his hand, and when I took it, we stood in front of an abandoned playhouse. It was nearly all boarded up. I could see a broken window under one of the boards. The paint was collecting greenish mildew. The old neon sign above the door was cracked and looked as if it could easily fall from where it was precariously perched.

The beggar extended his arm, hand up, pointing toward the doorway.

"It's closed," I said.

"Only if you dream it to be."

In a blink, the theater was alive. The glass was repaired, the boards were gone, the paint was fresh, and the neon sign was firmly hanging and beaming the words: *This Moment Only: Who Am I, Really?*

"The answer is within," said the beggar. He snapped his fingers and we were seated in the seventh row, in the center. The room was dark but for an illuminated, empty stage in front. The light from it allowed me to make out a few faces from the seemingly hundreds that were there, including Skye's, who was next to me, holding my hand. Jean was in front of us and turned to address me.

"So, Scott, how ready are you to finally lose your mind?" she said, with a beam as bright as the neon sign outside.

The beggar then whispered into my ear. "Close your eyes. Count to three, and open them again. When you do, you will experience Absolute Truth."

I closed my eyes in anticipation of seeing a miracle. What will I see? I don't know and I have no expectations. I'm not attached to anything. I'm just ready—ready to open my eyes to an even deeper reality. Funny, life's most important question is about to be answered, yet for the first time in my life, I'm patient and quite content just sitting here, eyes closed—if need be, for eternity.

Surreal and perfect. I'm smiling the kind of smile people have when they meet their soul mate for the first time and just know they have been, and will be, together, forever.

1 . . .

I am ready.

2 . . .

What a journey . . .

. . .

When I opened my eyes, I was on the stage, looking out into the audience, all of whom I knew. They were giving me a standing ovation, led by Greg, who stood in the very front row. The entire group then put their hands into prayer position, brought them to their chests, and bowed, namaste style. I took a deep breath and returned the bow. The crowd began chanting: "Speech, speech, speech."

As twenty-three pairs of chromosomes determine my physical essence, I shared who I really am, my Absolute Essence, with twenty-three words . . .

"I Am Awareness. I Am Acceptance. I Am Knowing. I Am Presence. I Am Freedom. I Am white light refracted into all beings."

Each of the audience members stood bathed within a unique hue, and I saw my *Self* through the blend of their colors.

All heaven then broke loose as Paula played her cello to an upbeat Springsteen song, while Chris beatboxed and Jean sang along. Karine looked fondly at me as she danced with Nowell, whose red suspenders were barely visible under his tuxedo. Lennon stood in the aisle, smiling at Damon and Ava who were holding hands and looking delightedly at one another. My mother and father, both wearing fisherman hats, cheered like the proud parents they were. Eric and Rose stood with their arms interlaced; Larry embraced Ginette with one arm and pointed his finger toward me with the other, mouthing the word "you" as he did so. Tom Reynolds, Alex, Greg's partner, as well as many others from my journey were all applauding wildly. The man with the black cap, now dressed in pale blue, winked at me. The beggar waved a ten-dollar bill my way, and Skye blew a kiss in my direction.

All the colors within the audience grew in intensity and turned to pure white—One light. I closed my eyes to more clearly see and experience the miraculous moment.

When I opened them, I was in my office. I watched as the time on the clock changed from 11:10 to 11:11. A brilliant bright light coming from outside my window began reflecting off the clock's face.

I again closed and reopened my eyes. I now stood on the other side of the street, looking into my office. There was a blank cardboard sign in my hand and a bucket on the ground in front of me.

 ONE IDEA AWAY

This book is meant to be lived, not just read.

How can you uncover and live the life of *your* dreams?

Join the One Idea Away community to access free resources to further explore and integrate the high conscious concepts presented in this book.

To get started,
visit: www.OneIdeaAway.com/dream

What you can uncover within the One Idea Away community:

- Online programs to help you incorporate the book's concepts into your life
- Discussion questions and a guide for creating your own book group
- Guided meditations based on the five portals
- Author interviews
- Uncovering the Truth dream journal
- An ever-expanding library of articles, research, videos, and podcasts
- Listings of upcoming retreats and other events in your area
- A directory of Certified Professional Coaches to help you accelerate your learning
- Information on becoming a Certified Professional Coach
- And much more

Start living the life of your dreams at
www.OneIdeaAway.com/dream!